DANGEROUS RED FLAGS

MY LIFE AS A BORDER PATROL AGENT

EUGENE DAVIS
WITH
AUBREY M. HORTON

LIBRARY OF CONGRESS
CATLOGUING-IN-PUBLICATION DATA
on file

ISBN: 978-1794207851
ASIN: B07MMP45HC

First Edition -- 2019

To my family for all of the missed birthdays and holidays when I had to spend long periods away from home on various details.

- 1 -

Forty-nine years ago, I never imagined I would be involved with stopping terrorists from entering the United States. Nor did I ever think that one day I'd be supervising a team of officers to prevent a fanatical bomber from killing innocent Americans or that a group of law enforcement agents, whom I'd worked with, would help track down a serial sniper.

But eventually my career was punctuated by those types of high-profile cases. Along the way, I was asked to testify before several Congressional committees in regards to illegal immigration and how our country's borders could better be protected.

Yet in 1970, I had no idea that was where my career path would take me. Back then, when I was twenty-five years old, my father had sent me a newspaper clipping. It said the Border Patrol was hiring people. At the time, all I knew about the Border Patrol was that it was a federal job and that its agents started as GS-7s with salaries of $8582.

As a child I had always wanted to be in law enforcement, but I had never heard anything about the Border Patrol. So I took the Immigration Patrolman Inspectors Test on May 6th, 1970. I scored a 90 out of a 100. A couple of months later, I was then called in for a physical exam and an oral interview in Idaho. In those days all of the new hires had to do an oral board with two Border

Patrol chiefs, where they would ask you three hypothetical questions.

So I showed up in Pocatello, Idaho. That day there was only one other guy besides myself who was there for an interview. He was kind of cocky. He said he knew a lot about the Border Patrol, and he told me a few things in regards to how they patrolled. As we were waiting to be interviewed, I told him I was worried I might end up stuck in a port-of-entry booth somewhere, checking cars. He said, "No, Border Patrol agents are mobile. They spend a lot of time driving around, searching for aliens trying to cross into the country illegally."

After we waited for about twenty minutes, the two of us were then sent into another room for our interviews. We were first told that the Border Patrol didn't hire any women agents. Again, this was in 1970; and it would be another five years before a woman officer was eventually brought onboard.

The two chiefs interviewing us next explained a little bit about the job, before they asked if either one of us knew anything about the Border Patrol.

I said, "No, I don't know anything about it."

The guy sitting beside me said, "Well, I know a lot about the Border Patrol. My brother was in the Border Patrol, and last year I went down south and rode with him on a shift one night."

The senior chief who was interviewing us then asked the other guy, "You said your brother *was* in the Border Patrol. Where is he now?"

"Oh, he promoted out and went to Customs."

When the cocky guy blurted that out, I saw the two chiefs who were sitting across from me at the table look at each other and shake their heads. Back then, Customs would hire almost every agent that wanted to transfer out of the Border Patrol.

I was next asked three situational questions by the two chiefs who were probably GS-12s or GS-13s. Those two guys had decades of experience on the border. One of them turned to me and said, "Okay, you and your partner are out working a night shift, and you come across a group of Chinese men who are being smuggled into the U.S. by a guide. All of a sudden, the guide takes off running; and your partner dashes after him. Now you've got fifteen Chinese left where you are. What are you going to do to control the situation?"

I swallowed hard and said, "Well, I guess I would tell the rest of them to sit down."

"Oh, you speak Chinese, do you?"

"No, sir. But I think I could gesture with my hands and get them to sit down."

"Okay, let's say they sit down. Then two of them get scared. They jump up and take off. What are you going to do now?"

I bit my lower lip and said, "I guess I'll stay right there because I've only lost three of them so far."

"Aren't you going to draw your gun?"

"I might. But I'd only do that as a last resort."

"Okay, let's say you draw your gun. That scares five of them, and they take off. Now what are you going to do?"

"Well, I certainly wouldn't shoot at them. I wouldn't fire my gun. So I guess I'd radio in and ask for assistance and get some help to come there and round them up."

The two chiefs nodded their heads when they heard me say this because that was the right answer. They then asked me a second question, which I also answered correctly. Yet the third question they asked me was even more interesting than the other two. On the last one they put me in a situation where I was on a passenger train, doing a border check. They told me I had found a guy who was illegally in the country, and the word was that a smuggler had brought him in on the train, and then the two of them had split up.

"Okay, so you find the alien on the train. Then after you determine he's illegal, how do you find the other guy who smuggled him in?"

I paused and thought about it for a moment and said, "Well, I guess I would talk to the porter."

"Okay, you talk to the porter, but he doesn't know anything. Then what do you do?"

"I guess I would then try talking to some of the other passengers. I think that might work."

"Alright, let's say you do that, but nobody knows anything. Can you think of something else you'd do?"

I thought about it for a moment and said, "I'm sure the alien would have a train ticket on him. So I'd check the other passengers' tickets since there's a chance that one of the tickets above his number or one of the tickets below his number would belong to the smuggler." I said that because I thought the train tickets might have been issued in consecutive order with corresponding numbers.

The assistant chief nodded his head and said, "Yes, that's right. You answered the question correctly."

So that's how I passed my interview.

As I was leaving the room, they wished me well and told me I'd done pretty good on the oral test. This was in September. Then later—on February 8th, in 1971—I got a phone call. It was someone from Western Union, and they read me a telegram that said I'd been selected for a conditional appointment as a Border Patrol agent and would be hired on as a GS-7 for service along the Mexican border. I was told to report for work on February 22nd, which would be in two weeks. That meant I only had two weeks' notice to put my affairs in order.

Now, since I hadn't expected this to happen that quickly, I had to go borrow some money because I needed the extra cash to cover my travel expenses so I could attend the Border Patrol Academy. They also had assigned me to a duty station in Chula Vista, California, which meant I first had to spend three days there—where I was initially sworn in as a federal officer. I next had to buy my own uniforms, which cost me $125. They later reimbursed me for that out-of-pocket expense.

Then after I'd officially come onboard, I rode with another recruit from Chula Vista to Los Fresnos, Texas, where I spent sixteen weeks at the Academy, which was outside of Brownsville. There were just over one hundred of us who'd showed up for the start of that training class. And once I'd completed all of my courses at the Academy, I returned to the Chula Vista station; and for the next ten months—I worked four days a week as a trainee. In other words, my training still continued on for one day each week while I performed my duties as a new Border Patrol agent.

In regards to the other hundred trainees that I had started out with at the Academy—by the time I had finished my initial ten months, we had already lost about 20% of the class due to the fact that they had failed out.

And that washout rate seemed to have been about average. At the Academy we were taught the equivalent of three years of college Spanish. Everything had to be grammatically correct. And we had to learn this in sixteen weeks. I'd never studied so hard in my whole life. We had two-man rooms in an old barracks that had been built in a former Naval base. My roommate was an ex-highway patrolman from Texas.

Needless to say, I found the Border Patrol Academy to be quite interesting. I thought our group of trainees was somewhat like the guys you'd find in the French Foreign Legion. We had all kinds of people from a variety of backgrounds. Each morning we'd wake up at 7 o'clock, and our classes would start at 8 o'clock. Then we would stay in school until 4 o'clock in the afternoon. It was a long day.

We studied Spanish, immigration law, and nationality law. We also had firearms training, along with a regimen of physical exercise. Plus, every night we'd have a study assignment, which might include some Spanish-grammar homework. It was a tough schedule.

The Academy wasn't easy, especially for someone such as myself since I'd never spoken a word of Spanish before I'd been hired on as an agent. It took me a while to learn the language, and the hardest part was memorizing all of the vocabulary. In ten months you had to be fluent in Spanish in order to graduate.

Then later, when I got back to the Chula Vista duty station, we had a post-Academy training officer, and we had to pass a five-and-a-half-month exam and a ten-month exam. So that meant we had to be tested on forty questions in order to fulfill the training requirement.

For example, someone would role-play and act like he was an illegal alien who'd been apprehended. We'd have twenty questions that we'd have to memorize in Spanish, such as: "What's your name? What's your address? What's your date of birth? Where are you from? How'd you get here?" Those were the questions you'd ask in Spanish since everyone would initially start out working on the southern border.

Learning how to question someone wasn't at all easy because the twenty questions had to be spoken in the correct tense with proper predicates. And you had to get 70% of the questions right on the test in order to get a passing grade. The instructors would wash trainees out if they couldn't cut it. I remember at my ten-month exam that there were four guys who'd washed out. And they were good officers, too; but they just weren't able to make it through the intense training.

-2-

I graduated from the 99th session of the Border Patrol Academy, which is now in New Mexico. I was then given a week's leave to go home and pick up my family for our move to Chula Vista. The Chula Vista sector was made up of seven patrol stations. There was the main Chula Vista station; there was another station in El Cajon, California; there was a station in Campo; there was a checkpoint in Temecula, California; there was a checkpoint station in San Clemente; and there were two interior stations, one in Oxnard and one at San Luis Obispo. The Chula Vista station was responsible for the Border Field State Park, which was right next to the Pacific Ocean. Then as you go east from there, we covered the 33-mile border that went all the way out to the Otay Mountains.

Back then, the Coast Guard was responsible for the ocean surveillance. Our units had no boat patrols at that time. But we did have an air unit. We probably had half-a-dozen pilots who flew Super Cubs, along with a few Cessnas. The Super Cubs were the main planes that coordinated with the agents on the ground in the field. Most of those pilots were World War II veterans. And the Super Cubs were really great. We worked a lot with them when we were out tracking aliens and doing our early-morning checks along the border. So in '71 we only had the Super Cubs and a couple of Cessnas. Then later, just before

I left in 1977, we got our first helicopter, which was a civilian version of the OH-6. This whirlybird was also known as the Loach, and the U.S. military had used it in Vietnam.

Now, because I was spending one day a week in school when I first started working at Chula, the thing that I most remember about that time was the training officer I had. He was a cantankerous guy with a down-to-business attitude. The journeyman agents who worked with him had told me that if I wanted to be successful and get ahead with no problems in his class—that I shouldn't get behind, nor should I try to get ahead. I was told not to raise my hand and ask a lot of questions. The journeyman agents also said I shouldn't go up to the training officer and try to brown-nose him or start any meaningless conversations. They told me, "Just do what we tell you, and you'll be fine."

So I really adhered to that. Then maybe about a month or so into the course, I was in the back of the room by myself. And all of a sudden I see the training officer making a beeline straight towards me with something in his hand. I looked to my left and to my right, and there was nobody else around. I thought I must've done something wrong.

The training officer then came up to me and said, "Mr. Davis, I've got a question for you."

"Yes, sir."

"I just looked at your personnel file. It said you graduated from high school in Afton, Wyoming, in Star Valley. Is that correct?"

"Yes, sir. That's correct."

"Well, let me tell you something about Afton, Wyoming. Last year my wife and I went on vacation to Yellowstone and the Grand Tetons. When we were heading back to California, my truck broke down; and I ended up spending four days in Afton."

I swallowed hard, not knowing what he might say next.

"Mr. Davis, I want you to know that those people in Afton, Wyoming, were the nicest people I've ever met in my life."

Whew, it was such a relief to hear him say that. And later, I often thought to myself, *What if my training officer had had a bad experience in Afton?* So I'll always remember the day he'd said that to me.

In regards to our regular duties as Border Patrol agents, there were a lot of what we called sign-cut roads in the area that we patrolled. These were dirt roads that ran parallel to the border. And back then, there was very little fencing along the Mexican border, although we did have some barbwire that ran through the sector near our station at the port of entry in San Ysidro. To clarify, everything west of there was considered the west side; and everything east of there was considered the east side. So W-1 on our patrol maps would be right at the port of entry on the west side. E-1 would be the area just east of the port of entry. The next area over was W-2, and so on—clear out to W-15, which was right at the beach.

On the east side you went from E-1 to a bunch of canyons and scrubland. Spring Canyon and Dead Man's Canyon were also over there. So it ran E-3, E-4, E-5, E-6, E-7—all the way out to the Otay Mountain Road. To cover our patrol beats, we drove Jeeps and International Scouts.

When I was training, one of the first things we did at the beginning of an evening shift was to go out and do a tire drag. We would hook some old tires together and drag the dirt roads. We'd get in an International Scout and pull the tires behind us. All of our vehicles had specially mounted lights. You'd flip a switch to turn the spotlights on at night, and that would shoot a beam of light across the road in front of you. Those high-intensity vehicle lamps really helped us find tracks in the dirt. Plus, the Border Patrol was quite famous for having really good mantrackers, too.

I remember in the evenings, after it had turned dark, I'd get in a vehicle and drive the dirt roads, looking for tracks. I could identify an individual by the marks the bottoms of his shoes made in the dirt. If I found a set of shoeprints—I'd call my partner on the radio since we worked alone in single-man units. I'd say to my partner in the other unit, "I've got a running-w sole headed north . . . or a Nike logo or whatever."

My partner would then check the road north of me and try to pick up the tracks in his location. If he verified the same set of shoeprints in the dirt, I'd skip over him and drive to the next parallel road and look for tracks there. If we got a set in-between us, the last person to find the tracks would get out and use a flashlight to follow the tracks. We'd mostly come across groups of aliens who were being led across the border by a guide.

I'd also like to point out that when I first started working for the Border Patrol in '71, almost everything we had, such as our two-way radios and the other equipment we used, was very primeval. Then things began to change. For years—sign-cutting, following people, or getting in front of them was the primary way we caught illegal aliens. But once we started getting some of the new technology that was coming out of Vietnam, such as electronic sensors, our surveillance methods incrementally improved. We soon had buried sensor lines set up on the east side of what we called Otay Mesa; and we also had sensors put in on the west side, starting at W-7. Plus, we were given specially outfitted Suburban-type vehicles to perform this type of work. If a patrol agent got assigned a sensor vehicle, he'd go out and physically hook into one of the microphone lines. He'd then sit at that location and listen for activity. And because the mics were super sensitive, he'd actually hear footsteps.

Now, let's say you were hooked up to lines 15 through 20, and all of a sudden you heard a sound on 15. An agent would know exactly where a sensor was buried. So he'd get on the radio and say, "I've got foot traffic on fifteen."

The other officers would then quickly loop north of that location and try to intercept the border crossers.

A couple of years later, we started getting magnetic sensors, which we would set up in places that we thought we had drive-throughs coming across in cars. And it wasn't long before we also had laser sensors and infrared sensors that alerted us to illegal crossings. So working with all of that new technology really gave us a much needed advantage.

It should also be noted that this network of sensor lines had its limitations, since we could only connect into one of these surveillance systems per a limited range of about a mile or so in each location. That meant when we started a night shift, we'd pick an area that we thought would have the most crossings. Of course, I think the smuggling guides eventually figured this out and would try to avoid the sensors.

I remember an incident that happened on the west side one night. An agent—who was operating a sensor unit—got out of his vehicle to do something, and he saw someone walking towards him, carrying a backpack. Now, this particular Border Patrol agent was kind of naïve because the stranger walking towards him suddenly pulled a pistol on him.

The alien then took the agent's gun from him and handcuffed him to a power pole. He threw the agent's .38 Special into the bushes. He then aimed a semiautomatic at the agent and pulled the trigger.

But thank goodness his handgun misfired. It wouldn't work. The alien took off and left the Border Patrol agent handcuffed to the pole.

Now, back when this happened, we'd have an hourly safety check on each shift since some of the agents would be assigned still watches with binoculars or they'd be put on roving patrols. So every hour the radio operator would do a safety check. If one of the guys had fallen asleep, someone would have to be sent out to check on him.

Anyway, the agent who'd been handcuffed to the power pole didn't answer his safety check. And luckily, it didn't take long to find him. Then a couple of our agents quickly discovered the tracks of the alien who'd tried to kill him, and they caught the guy pretty fast. So that incident served as a heads-up as to how truly dangerous our work was on the southern border.

Back then we also had some nights when we didn't apprehend anyone, even though the majority of our agents were assigned to the night shift. In the early '70s—we had three basic shifts. There was an 8 a.m.-to-4 p.m. dayshift. There was a 4 p.m.-to-midnight shift. And there was a midnight-to-8 a.m. shift. These three shifts gave us our 24-hour coverage. And on a lot of our night shifts, at the very most, we maybe had ten agents on duty, working out of the Chula Vista station.

As time went on we developed another shift. We called it the lay-in shift, and it usually started at 6 p.m. But the hours of the lay-in shift would sometimes vary. One week it might be from 6 p.m. to 2 a.m., then another week it'd be 7 p.m. to 3 a.m. The lay-in shift was utilized as an added emphasis to work areas that we expected to have heavy traffic on. A Border Patrol agent could be rotated to any shift; and he'd normally be assigned to one particular shift for two weeks in a row. My personal favorite was either the 4 p.m.-to-midnight shift or the lay-in shift. Needless to say, everybody wanted to work the shift which had the most activity. We all liked the action, and the lay-in shift was when we'd usually get a lot of traffic coming up from Mexico.

Now, to me, working those rough-terrain areas for the Border Patrol was a one-of-a-kind type of job. Then as the years progressed, we eventually got sensors down in the canyons, which meant we could plant ourselves on a trail and wait for the illegals to try to slip by. Of course, when I first started out, I was kind of nervous and scared. I knew it was dangerous work. But as the weeks went on, I got used to the area and to the people I was working with. The fear pretty much left me, and I soon became more aggressive.

One of my friends who I was working with at the time had been a Marine in Vietnam. And I remember him telling me that he thought we had to acclimate to our jobs somewhat similar as to what he'd experienced in the Marine Corps. He told me that when he'd started out in Vietnam—he was really, really uptight and tense. But as time went on, he said he'd gotten to know the terrain, he'd gotten to know the people, and it had become more of a regular job.

In addition to line watch and still watch, we also had a team of two to four guys who were assigned to a transportation shift each night. They would check the airport and bus stations in San Diego. We'd get a lot of illegal aliens who'd make it across the border; and they'd then take public transportation—either a bus, a train, or an airplane. For such transportation checks, we usually worked in plain clothes. Also, another thing we did in San Ysidro over at E-1, which was just east of the port of entry ... every night we would have a train which would come in from Mexico that we would have to check.

And you'd be amazed at what we'd find. We'd search the engines and the boxcars, and sometimes we'd pull twenty-five or thirty aliens off a train that they were attempting to ride into the U.S. We'd have to check all of the voids and empty spaces. I remember one time we were checking the freight yards in San Diego because a lot of illegals would jump trains there and ride them north. They'd hop up in the boxcars.

Then one night I was horrified when I found a dead body. The guy's hand, arm, and head had been cut off by a train's wheels after he'd slipped down onto the rails to hide and hadn't heard the railcar being pulled forward. A number of times over the years I'd seen guys get in train cars that were loaded with steel beams and then the load would shift. So like the hobos in the Great Depression—anytime someone hopped a train, there was always the chance that something could go wrong.

Years later, when we used to go to Oregon on immigration details, we'd work with the railroad police, which the hobos called railroad bulls. We'd talk to the bulls and to the hobos, and sometimes we'd get tips on where to look for the illegal aliens who were riding inside the trains.

Also, when we worked with the Mexican authorities, we'd sometimes have problems. For some reason, we never had a good relationship with the *Federales*. We didn't feel we could trust the *Federales* because there was a lot of corruption in the Mexican government.

I remember that it was really heartbreaking when we'd apprehend certain groups of aliens. We called those we caught who were not Mexicans—OTMs, which stood for "Other Than Mexicans." And back then we'd get a lot of people from Central and South America. Such migrants had traveled up through Mexico, where they'd hook up with some of the guides who they called coyotes. It was quite sad because there was a lot of violence along the Mexican border with the U.S.

In those days a coyote would charge someone $150 to go to Los Angeles. That was the per-person rate. And some nights we'd get a guide who'd only be moving three or four people by himself. Then on another night we might come across a guide with a group of fifteen or twenty aliens. But usually if we got big groups like that, the coyotes would split them up into two groups. And that created a real problem because sometimes we ended up with parents without kids or kids without parents. So one group might get through, and the other group would end up being apprehended. Then we'd have to hold them in custody and figure out what to do with the broken-up family.

I'd also like to point out that we'd often run into the same coyotes over and over again. We had an ID index that we would use to prosecute them with so they'd get some jail time. For the first offense, they might get 30 days. Then later, the longest sentence they'd get would be 179 days. This was done because if a person were sentenced to serve a jail term of 180 days, they'd be eligible for a release in 60 days. Whereas if a person received a sentence of 179 days, they'd have to then serve their full 179 days.

Now, the reason the sentencing was handed out in this manner was because we had a magistrate in San Diego who we called Hanging Harry. And, in all honesty, he was an interesting judge since he was a bit vindictive; yet he was always very fair, too. We really liked Harry due to the fact that he took immigration law so seriously. The first time he might be lenient with a guy and give him 10 days or 15 days. But if the same guy appeared before Harry a second time, the coyote would get a couple of months. Then if he stood in front of Harry a third time, the guy could count on getting the maximum sentence of 179 days.

I remember one time I was assigned to our special anti-smuggling unit, which handled human-smuggling cases that were sometimes associated with safe houses. I was in court with a couple of other Border Patrol agents who were doing arraignments in front of Hanging Harry. As we were just getting ready to start a proceeding—this young guy, wearing a suit and tie, walked into the back of the courtroom. He said, "Your Honor, my name is so-and-so. I'm a DEA agent. I'd like to approach the bench, Your Honor."

Harry said, "Okay, step forward."

The young guy then walked to the front of the courtroom and said, "Your Honor, I've got a man who's scheduled for arraignment for smuggling marijuana. But I'm way back on the docket. I've noticed that you've scheduled a number of simple immigration cases ahead mine, which are just border-crossing cases. They're not important cases like my case. Your Honor, I really need to be somewhere else, and I was wondering if I could move to the head of the line."

Harry lowered his glasses on his nose and said, "Young man, let me tell you something. Your marijuana case is not a priority for me. The marijuana has already been confiscated and burned. It's gone. But immigration cases can go on for generations. The most important cases I have before me are immigration cases. So I'm moving your arraignment time. I'm putting it at the end of the list."

That was a day I'll never forget. It warmed my heart to see that DEA agent get his comeuppance.

Now, once the illegal aliens had been sentenced, they were then sent to a county jail in San Diego. There was also a jail over in Arizona that was used for such cases, too. Plus, our anti-smuggling unit had come up with a special fingerprint method to handle the aliens because they'd frequently change their names. The illegals didn't have driver's licenses, and they'd use fake names when we questioned them. Likewise, a guide wouldn't have an ID or any paperwork on him, either. Most of the human smugglers carried absolutely nothing on their person. But the marijuana drug smugglers were different. We'd frequently find weapons on those guys.

Also, due to the Mexican border's rough terrain, it turned out that most of the guides were little river rats who knew the area quite well. They would work with the smugglers and guide them through. Of course, sometimes it was hard to tell who was a smuggler and who was a guide.

One thing we did, at least for a while, was look for guys who had long fingernails on their pinky fingers. When we'd catch a group of aliens, we sometimes at first wouldn't know who the guide was unless the other aliens would tell us. So we started running across guys who had a long fingernail on one of their hands. For some reason, this was a guide thing. It was machoism. It was a cultural thing. But that fingernail signifier eventually faded away after a while.

Not long after that, our anti-smuggling unit came up with a special fingerprint method, which functioned as a primary-print classifier. The way this worked was—we'd run a set of prints, and we had a formula for counting the number of whirls. We had a system we'd use when we caught a guy that we suspected was a guide. We'd take a picture of him, and let's say his fingerprint classification was a 10/16. We'd next go to the fingerprint files, check the 10/16 category, and look for a matching photograph. That's the way we could confirm a guy's identity from his thumbprint.

I remember a funny story that involved this process. One time we caught this guy who was a guide. But he claimed up and down that he wasn't a guide. He said, "I swear I've never been here before. You have the wrong person."

I then searched through our files and pulled out a photo. I showed it to him and said, "Is this you?"

He said, "No, sir. That's not me."

I stared him straight in the eye and said, "C'mon, don't lie to me. Yes, it is you. You're lying."

"No, that's my twin brother. He looks just like me."

Yeah, right. His twin brother, uh-huh. To this day I can't help but laugh when I remember him telling me that. So then I said, "Look, even though it's your twin brother, that's your fingerprints."

He raised his voice and said, "We're identical twins! We have identical fingerprints!"

I still crack up when I think about him telling me that. Yet I thought it was a nice try.

And since I was on the southern border for over six years, I've sometimes been asked if I ever got friendly with any of the guides/coyotes. When such a question comes up, I usually explain that most of the guides were pretty harmless. They were just doing it for the money. I remember one night in particular when we were working a shift around San Ysidro, surveilling a section we called the Loading Docks area, which included an upper-and-lower part. At that location there were a series of little hills that we referred to as the Loading Docks Lower. Some actual freight docks sat at the bottom of this area, and there were a couple of companies that would load up timber and other types of cargos from their warehouses. That's why we called it the Loading Docks.

Anyway, we'd get a lot of aliens who would come through the E-3, E-4 canyons. They'd then make their way back into San Ysidro, where a guide would have a load car waiting for them on the American side of the border. It was fairly common for a guide to have a load car parked near where he'd guided a group of illegals into the U.S. It was also really frustrating for us to find such cars since the same ones would be used over and over again. And that's when we began documenting those vehicles in a Rolodex after we'd busted a load of illegal aliens. Regrettably, that's all we could do since we had no authority to seize a car.

I remember one night in particular when we were working in the Loading Docks area. We'd already apprehended a couple of groups that had tried to come through, and we had this guide in custody who was watching us do our apprehensions. Suddenly, he got excited and said to me, "This is fun. Can I help you guys? Can I help you catch 'em?"

Smiling, I shrugged my shoulders and said, "Yeah, go ahead." So I uncuffed him, and this guide took off.

The guy ran over and hid in the bushes across from us. Then a little while later, he abruptly stood up when he saw another group trying to cross in. He waved at them, called them over, and said in Spanish, "Over here, my friends! Over here!"

They waved back and quickly walked toward him. He then guided them straight into us, and everyone started laughing. This guide did that three or four times. But he wasn't currying favor or asking for any sort of special treatment. He was just having some fun.

Also, at that time there were a variety of different nationalities that were coming across the border. We were getting a lot of the OTMs—"Other Than Mexicans"—flooding into the U.S. And sadly, many of them were carrying all of their life savings in cash, which sometimes they would give to their guides. And what compounded the problem when we'd apprehend the OTMs was the fact that we didn't trust the Mexican officials, i.e., we didn't trust the *Federales* very much.

So after we'd apprehend the Other Than Mexicans, we knew immediately—when we were interrogating them and filling out the paperwork . . . we'd quickly realize that they weren't from Mexico. We could tell by their dialect. Their Spanish was absolutely perfect, whereas most of the people we caught from Mexico, such as from the Chiapas and Durango areas, spoke with an indigenous dialect and used colloquialisms that were specific to their Mexican Native American cultures. Conversely, when we interrogated the Central and South Americans, they always used grammatically correct sentences. So we pretty much knew which aliens were from Mexico and which ones were lying to us.

But then to confirm our suspicions in order to be able to correctly document their nationality, we'd ask the OTMs a few questions in Spanish such as:

"Who is the president of Mexico?"

"*No sé.*" ("*I don't know.*")

"What color is the Mexican flag?"

"*No sé.*"

And especially with the women, we'd say to them, "Look, we know you're not from Mexico. Please tells us which country you're actually from." We did this because, if they weren't from Mexico, we'd have to send them to the processing center, which involved yet another set of paperwork and which meant they'd then have to be sent back to their country of origin.

So we'd explain to them what would happen if they didn't tell us the truth. "Okay, you're claiming you're from Mexico. Anyone we catch from Mexico, we have to drop off at the port of entry. You'll have to sign a voluntary departure, and then tomorrow you'll be sent back home. But if you're not from Mexico, that means we'll have to do a formal removal, and you'll then be deported back to your own country."

Yet the problem was, most all of them would lie and claim that they were from Mexico because they thought they would be able to quickly return to the border and illegally cross in again—after we'd released them to the Mexican authorities. But we'd try to warn them, especially the women. We'd tell them/beg them almost: "Listen, I'll tell you what's going to happen to you. We're going to take you down and turn you over to Mexican Immigration. They're going to take you inside their building. They're going to sexually assault you. Then in an hour from now, I'll get a phone call; and they're going to ask me to: '*Come pick up these people because they're not from Mexico.*' "

And that's what would happen almost every time. There was nothing we could do about it. Even Mexican workers, who'd regularly go back home after they'd finished a job in the United States, would be shook down at the border when they tried to cross back into Mexico with their pockets full of cash. This would happen over and over again. Many Mexican Immigration officers would steal their possessions and their money and whatever else they might be carrying on them when they attempted to return home.

I remember one night on the lay-in shift—I saw two uniformed Tijuana P.D. officers locked up inside a holding cell at the Border Patrol station. These Mexican policemen had come across the border; they'd busted a group of illegals; and they'd robbed them. The two officers had had no qualms about breaking the law so as to line their own pockets. Things such as that happened on a regular basis.

We also had another problem with the Mexicans we'd apprehend. What would happen was—soon after we would kick them back across the border—they'd wait a few days and try to come through a second time since most of them were from the interior of Mexico.

Then when they would attempt to cross in again, they'd use a different name. They'd make up an alias. And in order for us to keep accurate records, we needed to know the actual number of apprehensions we were getting, regardless of the false identities that a person might be using. In other words, we wanted to know if we were catching the same guy over and over again—or not. It was an important statistic that we had to nail down for our reports to be reliable. We needed to know if we were catching the same person five different times; or if it was, in fact, five different people.

So in 1974, a *rocket scientist*—who was working at one of our duty stations—came up with this great idea. He thought we'd be able to accurately gauge the number of crossings if we used indelible ink when we fingerprinted each illegal alien. This meant they wouldn't be able to wash the ink off their fingers. Then if we caught them again, we'd know from the ink stain that they'd already been kicked back once before. And this was a year or two before we'd begun using that fingerprint/photo method that I've already explained.

Anyway, what soon happened when we took the undocumented aliens back to our office to process them—the guys we had already fingerprinted started scribbling graffiti on the walls with the indelible ink. And we also had a second problem when the lid would come off an ink bottle in an agent's pocket. All of a sudden his shirt would be ruined with a big ink stain.

Needless to say, we didn't use that type of ink for very long. Nowadays, with the advanced computer systems and the facial-recognition programs, our agents can easily determine which identities are fake and which are real.

Another problem that started to accelerate back in the early '70s was an increase in the border bandits. We started to have a bunch of what we called *border rats* who'd lay in at night. They would rape women, and they would rob people. Now, to be clear, these weren't guides. These weren't coyotes. These were border bandits who were trying to take advantage of the aliens that the guides were trying to smuggle into the country.

This meant that we had to deal with four different types of individuals on the border. We had the illegal aliens who were trying to enter the United States. We had the guides/coyotes who were being paid to bring the illegal aliens across the border. We had the backpackers who were trying to smuggle drugs into the country. And we had the border bandits.

So at night on the lay-in unit, what we started doing was—we'd wear serapes and jackets to disguise ourselves. We did this to lure the bandits over to us. We needed to try to curtail the increase in criminal activity. Our intelligence agents were coordinating with the *Federales*, which meant we did have a certain amount of official cooperation from the Mexican authorities in this effort.

One night five of us were wearing our serape disguises. It was dark outside, so it was pretty hard to tell who was who. We were working down in one of the canyons. Under our striped blankets, we wore regular jackets to hide our uniforms. We also were carrying some shotguns with us.

About an hour after we started our surveillance, we spotted four guys, cutting through the cacti. They looked over at us and thought we were illegals. As they walked towards us, one of our guys made the mistake of pulling out his shotgun. That spooked the group, and they split and ran.

One of our agents then dashed after them. He sprinted around a tall cactus, leaped forward, and tackled a bandit who was about eighteen years old.

We took the punk back to our office. He wasn't at all respectful, and we had to process an apprehension file on him. We needed his name, his date of birth, his parents' names, and where he was born.

As we were filling out the bandit's paperwork, two *Federales* showed up at our office to interrogate the kid because they were getting a lot of heat from all of the criminal activity along the border. The two *Federales* then walked into the room where another Border Patrol agent and myself were sitting at a table and asking the arrestee some questions. The *Federales* weren't in uniform. They were in plainclothes.

Easing down in a chair across from the kid, one of the *Federales* asked him a question in perfect English.

The kid smirked and made a smart remark because he thought he was talking to a U.S. officer.

Then when the *Federale* asked him another question, the kid leaned forward and spit on him.

Fuming—the *Federale* reached across the table, swatted him, and knocked him off his chair.

The kid rubbed his face and slowly got up off the floor. In English he said, "You cannot do that. I will sue you. You cannot do that."

The *Federale* smiled and said in Spanish, "No, punk. You won't sue me. I'm not from U.S. Immigration. I'm a Federal official from Mexico."

The kid's face turned white as a sheet when he suddenly realized he was talking to a *Federale*. He swallowed hard and said in Spanish, "I'm very sorry, sir. Please forgive me. I'm very sorry, sir."

Then the *Federale* said, "Our conversation's over. In about half an hour, after they finish processing you and bring you down to the border, you will be in my custody, punk."

A short while later, when we took the kid to the port of entry, there were four *Federales* waiting for him. We never saw that bandit again. Then, like a curtain dropping down on a stage, the criminal activity in that canyon for the next couple of weeks was nonexistent. The word had gotten out that the *Federales* were cracking down.

Now, to be clear, most of the illegal aliens we apprehended were very respectful. A lot of them had been *braceros*, and they were simply coming up from Mexico to do farmwork. When I was first assigned to the border in '71, the majority of the people who were coming across the border were former *braceros*—i.e., they were farmworkers. And most of those guys did what they were told and never gave us much of a problem.

-3-

One of the things that we'd begun doing when we'd lay-in—was try to find the load vehicles that the guides were using for their people smuggling. One night in the Loading Docks area, I was in my patrol vehicle; and I had a new trainee with me. We'd been using our binoculars to scan the scrub brush along the border. We'd then gotten out of our vehicle. In my pocket I had a list of license plate numbers of the load cars which we'd previously busted. The plate identifiers that we'd always look for would be cars from the Los Angeles area since a lot of the load cars would come from there.

Walking down the street, I suddenly noticed an old sedan, which was parked on a side street that ran parallel to the border. It had an L.A. license plate holder. We walked over to the car, and I looked in its window. I didn't see any keys in the ignition. Bending down, I ran my hand over the top of the right-rear tire; and I found a set of keys. That's when I immediately knew it was a smuggler's load car.

Turning to the new trainee, I said, "Okay, let's go hide behind those bushes over there and wait and see who shows up for this."

Twenty minutes later—we were sprawled out on the ground under a thorn bush, and I'm peering through the binoculars. Off a ways I see this guy come out of the shadows. He runs up to the car and stops. Leaning down, he sticks his hand in the wheel well and feels the tire. He can't find the keys.

Cursing, he walks over to a phone booth and dials a number. He talks on the phone for a few minutes, hangs up, then goes back over to the car.

I then got on my walkie-talkie and radioed another team of agents. They drove in a short distance down from us as our backup.

A couple of minutes later, I watched the coyote who couldn't find the keys hurry back over to a group of illegals that he'd led across the border; and we quickly swooped in and did the apprehension. After we had them handcuffed, I dangled the keys in front of the coyote's face and said, "Is this what you were looking for?"

He cursed under his breath.

In the mid-70s we were finding a lot of load cars parked near the border, and some of our guys were getting pretty frustrated when they'd see the same car over and over again. To cope with their frustration, a few of them would "commandeer" a car that they knew was being used, repeatedly, to transport illegals. One of our guys even grabbed a set of keys and drove a car up to Bonita and parked it in the Southwestern Community College's parking lot. It sat there for months before it was finally towed away.

A short time after that, another one of our officers began driving the load cars up into a canyon. He'd take a rock, put it on the accelerator, and throw the shifter into gear. He'd quickly jump back and let the car go over the cliff.

In a way, our work was sort of like going off on a hunting trip. And that's why our guys loved it. They absolutely loved the job. It was an adrenaline rush. You'd come to work early, and you'd talk to the guys who were going off-shift in order to learn what they'd had going on.

It was similar to what policemen had to deal with when they'd do their rotating shifts. You'd get into this let's-go-catch-'em mode.

In 1975 I remember one night I had this film writer who was riding with me. I don't recall if he was doing a TV series or what it was he was researching. Anyway, he'd gotten permission to ride with me, and we were out on the west side in an area we called W-7, coming off Smuggler's Canyon. That night there wasn't much moonlight, and I was notified that a sensor had been tripped. I told the writer we had time and that we were going to beat the illegals to the bottom end of the canyon.

So I pulled my patrol vehicle over and hid it behind some tractors. I then told the writer to run, and we ran into this big bunch of bushes. As we hunkered down on the ground, all of a sudden I heard these guys coming off the hill beside us. I had a regular jacket over my service jacket, which meant you couldn't see my uniform.

Anyway, this group of aliens snuck into the same clump of bushes that we were hiding in. We instantly froze and kept our mouths closed since we didn't want them to know we weren't illegals.

Then about three minutes later—a car pulled up, parked in front of us, and the driver got out. It was a load car. Now, what usually happened with the load cars was that the original driver would then act like he was a passenger. So instead of sitting behind the wheel when the car was driven into the interior, the original driver would tell one of the other illegals to drive the car. A coyote would use this ploy because he wanted to blend in. He didn't want the Border Patrol agents to know who he was if the car got pulled over.

So this load car pulled up near the bushes, and everyone ran over to the car. The film writer and I dashed along with them.

Then as the illegal aliens jumped inside the car, the two of us stopped a few feet away from it. I stared at the guy who was behind the wheel, stepped over to the driver's door, reached in the window, grabbed the keys out of the ignition, and turned on my flashlight. I pointed it at the coyote in the backseat and said, "Gotcha!"

The adrenaline was surging through me, and my heart was racing. But this was the type of unexpected situation that a Border Patrol agent would have to deal with quite frequently. To get the job done, you had to think on your feet. You had to quickly weigh the *risks* to your life versus the *benefits* of achieving a successful apprehension. That's how we made it work night after night. And by sheer happenstance, that film writer—who was riding with me—had picked a really interesting shift for his research.

In regards to the surveillance technology that was being transferred to us by the military, back during the Vietnam War . . . I remember another time when I was working a different section of the border. Not only had we begun deploying ground sensors, which would alert us to any foot traffic, but we'd also been given Starlight Scopes, i.e., large-and-small night vision devices.

So one night on the lay-in shift, we had an agent who was surveilling the west side. He was scanning the border with a big Starlight Scope. Then he suddenly spotted a guide leading a group of four backpackers, which meant they were smuggling drugs. Also, I'd been off for a week on annual leave, and that was my first night back at work.

When I heard our agent radio in what he'd spotted, I got out of my vehicle. I realized that I had parked right in front of the spot where these aliens would be coming across the border. And that's when I noticed a fence line that ran down through the field and abruptly made a dogleg. Across from the fence was a big bush, and I quickly hid inside it. Then I watched as this group of backpackers proceeded to hike along the fence, turn, and make the dogleg.

Peering through my binoculars, I suddenly saw them stop; but I noticed that the guide continued on by himself. He'd left the four backpackers behind him. And that's when I started to get a bit worried because he was walking straight towards me.

I tried to stay calm because I was stuck in that bush. Yet there was nothing I could do as I watched him crawl into my hiding spot.

Sucking in a deep breath—I slowly eased my pistol out of its holster, rolled over, and knelt him down. I got on my walkie-talkie and said, "I have the four backpackers in sight. They're right up the road at the end of the fence which has a twisted-out dogleg."

A group of our agents then sped over there, and they apprehended the four backpackers. We then took them into the office to process them. And that night, for some reason, there was a lot of activity, a lot of people to be processed. Now, the thing was, we had lockup boxes where we'd stow our guns when we were processing our apprehensions. Also, on such a busy shift, it was pretty common, if all of the gun lockers were being used, that the late arrivals would simply unload their pistols and take out the ammo for safety purposes. Yet when I checked my gun, I saw that it was already unloaded. I'd forgotten to load my gun because I'd been off the week before. So I guess you could say I'd bluffed the coyote who'd tried to hide in that same bush with me since he'd had a knife on him.

Yes, indeed. Those were the kind of adrenaline rushes we'd frequently have to deal with. But luckily for us, because we were required to write up the paperwork on the people we had apprehended each night, that bit of office work actually sort of helped us wind-down from our shifts. Then once we'd finish with the paperwork, we'd go to the coffeeshop and brief the guys who were coming in on the next shift as to what had gone down on our shift.

Towards the end of my assignment at the Chula Vista station, which was in 1977, it wasn't uncommon for us to pick up a hundred and fifty people on a single 8-hour shift. Back then, the border crossings always tended to increase in the late summer and early fall due to the growing seasons for various crops. The majority of the aliens that we caught—and this goes back to the late '60s and the early '70s when the Bracero Program had ended—were agricultural workers. Also, in addition to our eyes-on-the-ground sector surveillance, another thing that we'd look for were certain vehicles (beside load cars), such as pickup trucks with Oregon and Washington State license plates. Our guys would nab a good many of the smuggling loads at the checkpoints. On Interstate 5, going north out of San Diego towards Orange County, near San Clemente and Temecula, they'd pick off a lot of the load vehicles.

But then a bit later, as time went on, we weren't just apprehending agricultural workers. We started catching illegal aliens who'd come across the border to do work in a variety of other jobs. I remember one night we caught some guys in a car, and there was another guy in the car's trunk. When we brought them in for processing, I talked to the guy who'd been hiding in the trunk and asked him what type of work he did in Mexico. He told me he was an upholsterer.

I said, "Oh, my mother was an upholsterer." We then had a really interesting conversation about how one goes about fixing up old furniture.

Anyway, after I finished his paperwork, he was returned to Mexico the next day. Then the following night, when I was working in a different area, we caught a group of eight aliens. They didn't give us any trouble. And as two of us were putting them in a van, all of a sudden I heard, "*Buenas noches, Señor Davis!*"

It was the upholsterer guy. I smiled, nodded my head, and told him he was going to have go back through processing.

And that's what happened. He was again sent to Mexico.

I was then off work for two days; and on my first night back, I was in a roving vehicle. We used such sedans on the east side and west side. So I got a radio call and was told that the California Highway Patrol had stopped a U-Haul truck on a traffic violation, just north of San Diego. The dispatcher also said there was a bunch of illegal aliens in the back of the truck.

Not wasting any time, I quickly drove up to where the truck had been pulled over. Then when I opened up the U-Haul's rear door, I couldn't see anything because it was really dark inside the truck's rear.

A voice said, "*Buenas noches, Señor Davis!*"

I can't help but laugh when I think about that upholsterer guy. I had caught him three times, but he wasn't bitter at all. He was quite a nice guy.

Now, I guess I should also explain that the Mexican border, in certain parts of Southern California, ran right up into the outlying neighborhoods of some of the little towns, such as in San Ysidro—which was smack-dab on the border and which was one of the places that we actually did have a fence which separated the two countries.

I remember we had a smuggling case that we called the Smyth house. A woman lived in the house; and at night illegal aliens would hide there. Then during the day, a guide would load them in a car. It was a safe house. So after we busted the place, we didn't have any more activity in that particular neighborhood for quite a while.

Also, I recall another case we had soon after that in one of San Ysidro's newer housing areas. A couple of our agents were tracking a group of seven aliens who'd crossed the border, and one of the agents had radioed in from a mobile unit. He said, "I think they're headed to the Del Sol area."

That night I'd been assigned to another mobile unit, and I knew the trail he was referring to since it went right into the Del Sol neighborhood, not far from the border.

The other two agents then drove to Del Sol and started looking for a load car. They knew where the trail entered the neighborhood, and they checked out the surrounding streets. That's when one of the agents spotted this car that was parked next to a house. The car had a Los Angeles license plate holder, and the keys were in the ignition.

Now, sometimes what would happen—if a guide knew we were staking out his load car—well, he'd just abandon it. In other words, he'd hide the group in a safe house and come back later with another car.

Anyway, after the Border Patrol agent had found what looked to him to be a load car that night, he'd hopped inside it and started it up. He then drove it down to where the trail came into the Del Sol area, blinked its lights a few times, and sat there and waited with the engine running.

But nothing happened.

Getting a little anxious, he then drove the car back to the house where he'd "confiscated" it, parked it out front, and waited another ten minutes—before he did the same thing a second time. And again, he drove the car over to the trailhead, blinked the lights, and nothing happened.

So after the agent had done this twice and he'd brought the car back to the house where it'd been parked, a guy walked out the front door and tapped on the car's window. He said, "I'm so-and-so. This is *my car*."

Smiling at the guy—the Border Patrol agent told him he'd made a mistake, explained who he was, and apologized.

The car owner scratched his head and replied, "Well, I was worried when I saw you leave the first time. But my brother told me it was just the Border Patrol and that you'd bring my car back."

I still chuckle when I remember what happened that night. It's a cautionary example of the cat-and-mouse game which we'd sometimes get caught up in. And even though we'd make those types of mistakes—they were, of course, unintentional. We were simply trying to do our jobs as best we could under the circumstances.

Also, back then, we never had any sort of counter-terrorism training, nor was there even a smidgen of concern at all for terrorists coming across the border from Mexico. It wasn't something we thought about. And this was because the U.S. had never had, up until that point, a terrorist attack that had been instigated by illegal aliens who'd been smuggled into our country.

Plus, to be clear as to the southern border's vulner-ability, we only became aware of the hand-chiseled smuggling tunnels a few years after I had later transferred up to the Canadian border. To the best of my recollection, I think the first time a smuggling tunnel had ever become a problem for us was either in the late '70s or early '80s.

I'd also like to clarify how we worked our shifts in the 1970s. Most of the time we were not partnered up. Normally, we'd be alone, in separate vehicles. And about 25% of the Border Patrol's employees were Hispanic/Latino. They were good officers and very dedicated. Of course, as with any such large organization, there were a few times that we had some officers arrested for being involved in drug smuggling. But the majority of our officers would never ever do anything such as that. If a recruit made it through the Academy and passed his ten-month exam, I think he felt the emotional bond of a tight brotherhood and immediately had respect for the other journeymen due to the intensity of those training courses and because he also knew they'd been through that same ten months of hell. Of course, it wasn't easy for the native

Spanish speakers to qualify to be patrol agents—simply based upon their language skills—because of the regulatory requirements to have to also learn the various immigration-and-nationality laws. During my whole career as a Border Patrol agent, I had nothing but praise and respect for most of my fellow officers. Ninety-five percent of the agents I worked with were the salt of the earth. They'd gone through the same training I had.

So if you ask me, I think that was one of the reasons the Border Patrol Academy had the reputation it did for being the toughest federal training facility when compared to the other agencies. Again, it was the academics of having to learn near-perfect Spanish and having to also come up to speed on the various immigration laws, etc. Indeed, people from all sorts of backgrounds were attracted to the challenge. One time I worked with a guy who had a PhD. He'd been a tenured professor and had gotten tired of the mundane lifestyle which he'd found himself bogged down in. So he'd joined the Border Patrol. And once he'd finished his training, he absolutely loved it. For him, I guess getting outside and driving around was a better fit per his personality than sitting at a desk every day and doing the same thing over and over again. When a patrol agent worked on the border, no two weeks were hardly ever the same.

Hence, in my opinion, the Border Patrol Academy is sort of the West Point of the Immigration Service. In other words, the Border Patrol has always functioned as the law enforcement arm of the INS, but its employees also perform a variety of other duties besides guarding our borders. The agency employs criminal investigators and immigration examiners who work in a number of our big cities, along with immigration inspectors who work at the ports of entry. So a lot of the employees who have ended up working various jobs for the INS—these officers first spent three or four years working for the Border Patrol before they had eventually burned out and had requested a transfer to another assignment. It's quite a demanding job which, soon or later, wears a person down. The agents love doing it, but it's hard to sustain the required intensity year after year. In one respect, I guess you could compare the mental focus to that of a pro athlete. An NFL player can only take so many hits on the football field before he finally has to call it quits. The psychological mind game is truly that intense on the border. It takes a lot out of you, emotionally, to constantly have to interact with a never-ending flood of illegal aliens.

Specifically, I recall back in 1973, a bunch of agents— including a number of my Academy classmates— requested transfers off the Mexican border because Chicago and Los Angeles were hiring dozens of new investigators. And, needless to say, that left us short-handed. Our manpower had been weakened considerably, and we knew there was a lot of people smuggling and contraband that was getting by us, like drug loads that we weren't catching.

So in '73 the Customs Service brought in a group of guys they called the Customs Patrol. And these officers ended up working in the same areas that we did, yet we had no real communication with them. Ninety-nine percent of them spoke no Spanish at all. For some reason, the higher-ups had dropped the ball; and these new guys hadn't had the language-skill training that all Border Patrol agents were required to have. This flaw was partly due to the fact that these new Customs Patrol agents had actually been initially employed as the very first sky marshals, which the agency had ended up disbanding. And so the D.C. administrators, who'd made this monumental mistake, had wanted to create some employment positions for those ex-sky marshals, and it was decided that they could perform similar duties as the Border Patrol.

Therein, when the ex-sky marshals had first been assigned to the border in '73, even though they were really inept, we knew—since there were so many drug loads flowing into the country—that these guys were going to take down some busts.

So four other Border Patrol agents and myself went to the patrol agent in charge and said, "Look, we're working ten hours a day. We're pulling regular eight-hour shifts, along with two extra hours of uncontrolled overtime. What about letting us change our shift time. Instead of us coming in at 8 o'clock in the morning, why don't you let us come in at 5 o'clock in the morning, and we'll work our U.O.T. before the shift?"

The patrol agent in charge agreed to the change in our start time and told us we could try it for two weeks.

We then came in early and deployed up on the Otay Mesa, where we knew a lot of the smuggling was going on. In three days we seized 1859 pounds of marijuana, 2.5 pounds of cocaine, and 4 automobiles. For our effort, the five of us received a letter of commendation, which went in our personnel files. It was dated October 19, 1973; and it was signed by Allen Gerhardt, who was the Chief Patrol Agent of the Chula Vista sector.

I knew Allen well because when I'd first come onboard, a chief was like a god to us new trainees. And so to backtrack a little—after I'd passed my five-and-a-half-month exam, I was working the dayshift down at a place we called E-1, right close to the railroad tracks, which was a still-watch position. The dispatcher had radioed me and said they were sending a unit down to replace me. I was instructed to come into the office. I had no clue why I was being called in from the field.

So I drove back to the station and walked into the office of the patrol agent in charge. He was sitting at his desk. The chief, Allen Gerhardt, was sitting across from him; and he had my personnel file in his hand. He said to me, "I've been going through your records, and I noticed you used to be a welder, is that correct?"

I said, "Yes, sir."

"Eugene, I have this special construction crew that's working on a project for me. I need some window screens welded. Do you think you could help me out for a couple of weeks?"

I nodded my head. I mean, I couldn't say "no" to the chief patrol agent. So I ended up working on that darn project for five weeks. Needless to say, my Spanish started to suffer. And since I thought I was wasting my time with that type of work, I finally went to the patrol agent in charge and told him, "I need to get back into the field. I was hired as a patrol agent, not as a welder."

And thank goodness my work assignment was then changed back to my regular duties.

-4-

Back in 1971 and 1972, when I first began working as a Border Patrol agent—there were nights that were pretty slow. On some of our shifts we didn't apprehend a single person. I remember one night I was sitting out in my vehicle, and it was quiet and nothing was going on. Then I heard someone key their radio, and an officer farted into his mic. But, of course, none of us knew who it was.

Then someone else did it—*intentionally*.

A couple of minutes later, it happened again. It quickly became a little-boy's game that kept going and going.

The next night I was working the midnight-to-8 a.m. shift; and the P.A.I.C.—i.e., the patrol agent in charge of that station—walked into the muster room (because we always had a muster at the start of each shift. And usually, you'd never see the P.A.I.C. on the midnight shift.)

Anyway, the P.A.I.C. said, "Alright, I've been told by radio that someone out there has been fartin' into the mics. Now, listen up. We're a professional organization. This isn't funny. I want it stopped right now. Do you guys understand what I'm saying?"

No one said a word. The room was totally quiet. You could hear a pin drop.

The P.A.I.C. then said, "Next time I'm going to bring my assistant with me. If this happens again, we'll find out who's doing it. We may have to smell the microphones."

Now, I know that sort of talk is hard to believe, but it really did happen. And I can't help but laugh when I think about the P.A.I.C. actually saying that. So back in the '70s, we'd have a little comic relief when we could. Such joking around helped relieve the tension the agents felt in regards to the stress they were under to do their jobs.

Also, I'd like to clarify a false impression that some people seem to have as to what our official duties actually involved. The majority of the aliens that we apprehended were not deported. Instead, most of the undocumented illegals that we caught on the border could, in fact, choose *"voluntary* departure." So it should be noted that this turned out to be something that most of the aliens actually agreed to.

For example, if an illegal alien told us he was from Mexico, then he could *voluntarily* agree to be sent back to Mexico. He would not be put in prison. He would simply be sent back to his own country. That's how "voluntary departure" was enforced. Congress had enacted the immigration laws, and the Border Patrol had been given the authority to uphold those laws.

So now, when certain political activists refer to our fellow Immigration and Customs Enforcement officers (i.e., ICE) as the "gestapo"—that's absolutely absurd. Such activists are just languaging inflammatory hyperbole to buttress their own agendas. To me, their exaggerated hot-button labeling rings hollow. Homeland Security is simply returning the undocumented aliens to their countries of origin. And, to the best of my knowledge, our officers are performing their duties with compassion and concern for the individuals they apprehend. We're the good guys, and we're enforcing the laws that Congress has enacted. That's what the Border Patrol and ICE agents are being paid to do. Our job is to protect U.S. citizens from harm by apprehending the undocumented aliens who have entered our country illegally; and this includes rounding up the foreign criminals and violent terrorists who've been smuggled across the border. That's the bottom line.

Also, as I've already pointed out, the OTMs—i.e., the Other Than Mexicans—were handled a little bit differently. To process them, we had to go through a formal hearing. Yet they, too, could choose to take a "voluntary departure." So, again, it'd be a misnomer to say that they were deported, because they could also choose to be sent back to their own country without having to go through a formal hearing before an immigration judge. Whereas if they did request a hearing and if an immigration judge did, in fact, declare them officially deportable, then they were removed from the country. And if that happened and if they later returned to the United States—such criminal activity would, at that point, be considered a felony. So being "formally" deported had serious legal implications.

Consequently, per U.S. statutory law, a lot of the illegal aliens would choose "voluntary departure" and thus would waive an immigration hearing. That meant in the future, if they did make another attempt at entering the country illegally and if they were then caught, a felony arrest wouldn't show up on their record, i.e., they wouldn't have that strike against them.

There's another interesting incident that happened one night when I was out working on the river bottom, close to the port of entry. For those who don't know the term, a "port of entry"—on our southern border—is an official checkpoint where the U.S. and Mexican governments stop travelers and verify they have the proper documents to cross into or out of the country. A port-of-entry checkpoint is also where we'd drop off the Mexican aliens we'd apprehended and who were then turned over to the Mexican Immigration officers after we'd finished processing them back to their country.

So on this particular night, I was teamed up with a partner. This was probably in April or May of 1976. We were in a patrol vehicle, and an infrared sensor had suddenly gone off. We thought that it'd been tripped by foot traffic. Of course, certain animals would also set off a motion sensor, too. Plus, I knew a good bit about these types of sensors since I'd once spent three months on a sensor detail, deploying them throughout that sector.

What we'd normally do after we'd set a sensor out— was that we'd then walk the trail that was cutting through the canyon where the sensor had been planted and time it so as to pick another spot to put out the next sensor. In other words, if we just got a single hit, that wouldn't be a very good confirmation of foot traffic. Or, to put it another way, the sensor might simply have been tripped by an animal. But then if we got a second hit, we knew that it was probably human foot traffic.

Now let me back up a little bit. At that time we had a lot of retired military people who were working for the Border Patrol. One was a gruff guy out of the Navy. I liked him, but he was sort of a funny person to work with. And since I had seniority, I made the important decisions because some nights we'd double up in a vehicle.

Here's what I didn't let get under my skin. If he was driving, that ex-Navy guy would pull up to the gas pumps; and he'd only wash his side of the windshield. When I watched him do this, I'd just chuckle and shake my head. It didn't matter to me if the bugs weren't cleaned off my side of the windshield. Like a lot of the guys, I had a sense of humor about those types of things.

Anyway, one night I was riding in a sedan with one of my classmates. Sensor #103 went off in the E-1 area, and the ex-Navy guy had radioed it in. He was near some railroad tracks that came out of the Loading Docks area and crossed into what we called the Travel Lodge Canyon. Up until that point, the night had been pretty quiet; and nothing had been going on. When I heard the ex-Navy guy radio in the sensor hit, I told my classmate to, "Pull over and let me out. Let's give him a little excitement."

And that's what my classmate did. He drove into a parking lot, and I got out. The ex-Navy guy was in another vehicle, and he couldn't see the spot we'd pulled into. From where he was—about all he could do was watch the sensor lights, look down the railroad tracks, and check to see if anyone was walking across them.

Hurrying away from the patrol sedan that I'd hopped out of... I then snuck in the back way, picked up a big piece of tumbleweed, and put it on my shoulders. I tried to make it look like I was carrying a backpack. I then ran across the tracks and tripped the sensor because I knew where it was.

It fooled the ex-Navy guy, and he radioed in, "Sensor 103 just went off."

My classmate radioed back, "Ten-four."

Running back to the sedan—I ditched the tumbleweed, jumped in the car, and we took off.

Then all of a sudden, we saw the ex-Navy guy running down the tracks, huffing and puffing. He was yelling into his radio, "BACKPACKER, BACKPACKER, BACKPACKER!"

Another unit quickly responded to his radio call and sped over to where he was. Then after the other unit had searched the area, they told him, "We can't find anybody. Are you sure you saw someone on the tracks?"

The ex-Navy guy started cursing and said, "Yeah, dammit! I swear I saw someone." Now, right at that spot next to the railroad tracks was a bunch of old road equipment. So the ex-Navy guy then crawled through each of those rusted-out machines because he wanted to prove he was right. Of course, he never did find anyone.

By the next morning, everyone in the unit had heard about the joke that had been pulled on him.

I also remember another night when a sensor had gone off, and one of our agents had caught this 12-year-old boy, who was trying to cross into the country by himself.

But the thing about this kid was—he wasn't a Mexican. He was from Guatemala. Three or four months earlier, there had been a massive earthquake in Guatemala. The boy had lost his mom and his dad and all of his brothers and sisters—with the exception of one brother who'd been living in Los Angeles when the earthquake had hit. So this 12-year-old kid had come all the way from Guatemala and had made his way up through Mexico to the U.S. border. He was trying to get to L.A. to find his older brother.

After the kid was caught by one of our agents, he was turned over to the ex-Navy guy. The boy was then put in a van and driven to the Chula Vista duty station. There he was questioned, and the ex-Navy guy made some calls. He tried to locate the kid's brother.

Luckily, he found him. And he did it relatively quickly because Los Angeles had Guatemalan neighborhoods where a lot of the immigrants knew each other. In a big city like that, it's common for people of the same nationality to live fairly close to one another. So the ex-Navy guy was able to get ahold of someone, and he was told that the kid's brother had come into the country illegally but had married a U.S. citizen and had gotten a green card. The ex-Navy guy had also been told that after the earthquake, the older brother had flown down to Guatemala and had just assumed that his younger brother was dead because everybody else in his family had been killed by the quake.

Then late that same night, after those phone calls had been made, the older brother drove down from L.A. to pick up the kid. At 8 a.m. we released the 12-year-old. It was such a sad story, but it had a happy ending. And it goes to show you that an ex-Navy guy might come across as a bit gruff, but underneath his outward facade is a heart of gold.

I'd also like to point out that our agents had to deal with many hardship stories such as that all of the time. I remember in 1983, when I went back down to the southern border on a 30-day detail as a journeymen

Border Patrol agent, it was really disheartening to discover that the bandit problem had gotten much worse. I mean, it had gotten pretty bad. We'd actually hear women screaming in the canyons, being assaulted by bandits. It would break my heart. Then when we'd try to find the women, a lot of times we couldn't track down where they were. Those canyon walls would play tricks on your ears.

One time on the west side when I was driving along a road that ran perpendicular to the border, I saw these two Mexican guys who were walking next to the road in front of me, and they looked like they were illegal. Then as I was putting them in the back of the patrol car, one of them said to me, "*Señor,* I need to tell you there's a *cuerpo* up on the hill."

A *cuerpo* was a dead body.

I got on the mic and told the dispatcher, "You need to notify the San Diego P.D. that we have a possible person down."

At about that same time, one of our Super Cub pilots was flying overhead; and he immediately dropped down over the fence and radioed back, "Roger that. There's a person on the ground, not more than two hundred yards from your vehicle."

Well, it turned out to be a 19-year-old kid. Someone had held his hands behind his back and had cut his throat. Sadly, we had a number of homicides such as that. We'd find dead bodies fairly frequently along the border. But that type of violence wasn't just limited to the illegals. We also had several of our agents who were wounded by backpackers. I remember three different instances of our guys getting shot by drug smugglers. Such backpackers, moving high-dollar loads, were much more dangerous than the coyotes. And, as I remember it, in the five or six years after I left the southern border, the Border Patrol had at least a half-dozen cases where bandits were killed in gun battles with our agents. Also, we didn't have bulletproof vests at that time. They were first issued to us when I'd come back up to the northern border in the early 1980s after I'd returned from a temporary assignment on the U.S.-Mexico border.

I also vividly remember what happened in 1973, when we had the big gasoline crisis. We'd go to work at night, and they would assign us still-watch positions. We were told to cut back on our driving because there wasn't enough gas for the vehicles. Our roving patrols were limited to still watches. They were rationing our gasoline.

So some of our guys started bringing siphoning hoses and five-gallon gas cans with them to work. Then when they found a smuggler's vehicle, they'd siphon out its gas tank and pour the gasoline into their assigned Border Patrol vehicle. This allowed them to be more mobile. On certain assignments a few of our guys even got more innovative. When they were sent to a river bottom, say down into W-2, they'd be given orders to do a still watch, which meant they were supposed to curtail their driving activity and stay in one place.

But the guys would get bored. They'd drive around, and then they'd back up their vehicles to roll back the odometers. In other words, when those International Scouts were driven backwards, it would reverse their mileage. So luckily for us, that national fuel crisis only lasted a few months.

When it came to border surveillance, we were really fortunate to have some very good air pilots. Many of them had flown for the military. Of course, at that time they mainly flew during daylight hours. They would begin their shifts really early in the morning when there was still dew on the ground. They'd then fly their Super Cubs low over the scrub brush, looking for fresh tracks or for groups of aliens. When they'd find them, they'd circle their plane.

Or if an agent was on foot and he came across some tracks, he'd radio it in and have a pilot fly overhead. I remember one morning when I was in the Otay Mountains on the east side. I was following some tracks on a truck trail. From the shoeprints in the dirt, it looked as though there was a group of four people ahead of me. I was pretty sure this group didn't have a guide since they were going the wrong direction. Sometimes we'd have small groups try to cross the border without a guide.

On this particular morning, I was sign cutting and had radioed in for a pilot to fly over and scout the area. Then as I was following the shoe tracks in the rough terrain, I suddenly heard a *BURR-BURR*.

It was a rattlesnake.

Back then I used to carry snake shot in my pistol. Usually, when I fired snake shot at close range, I wouldn't miss.

So I shot the snake, left it there, and got back on the tracks. Pretty soon, I found the four guys. Then as the pilot circled around overhead, I walked the illegals back down the truck road. Along the way, I reached down and picked up the snake by the tail. I did this because there was an agent I worked with who used to skin out rattlers. If anyone got a rattlesnake, he wanted it.

When I got the four aliens back to my vehicle, I dropped the snake into the front floorboard on the passenger side. It was still moving around, but I knew its squiggling was just a postmortem spasm.

Leaning his head in from the backseat, one of the illegals got nervous and said, "*Ay, caramba!*"

I tried to calm the guy down. In Spanish I told him that his friends and him didn't have anything to worry about. I explained that the snake wasn't going to bite them.

Then during the long drive back to the office, those four guys didn't say a word. Not a single word. I think that rattlesnake really had spooked them.

For the whole time I worked on the Mexican border, I don't remember any of our guys ever getting snakebit. We were always quite careful when we were out in the desert because we didn't carry antivenom with us. Whereas the biggest nuisance in those canyons at night were the cholla cactuses. If you bumped into a cholla, their sharp spines would stick into your leg. So we tried to avoid them. I was stuck a number of times. When that happened, I used my Buck knife to clip them off and pull the spines out. They were pretty painful.

Now, even though all of our pilots were really good, some of us began telling the higher-ups—around the end of the '70s—that what we really needed were helicopters. But the problem was, most of our pilots had only been trained to fly fixed-wing aircraft. That meant they didn't want us to transition to helicopters because they were only qualified to fly airplanes.

But we soon began getting a lot of Border Patrol agents who'd been pilots in Vietnam. After two years of service, they'd be released out of the Army; and these guys had the required training to fly helicopters.

Then in 1976 our duty station purchased its first helicopter, which was a Loach. This was the same model the hunter/scout teams had been using in Vietnam. So at that point we already had a number of helicopter pilots who'd been hired as patrol agents. They had thousands of flying hours, and we instantly became aware of how effective a helicopter was for our surveillance. At night we'd mount a big searchlight on the Loach. I flew three months as an observer, with a handful of different pilots. When we'd turn on that spotlight and scan its beam across the ground after sunset, it really helped us catch some of the smuggling groups that I'm sure we would've missed if we hadn't've been flying overhead in a chopper.

So as a result of the Vietnam War, the Border Patrol eventually ended up getting thirty-nine of the Loaches from the Army.

Of course, due to the shadowy environment along the border, we had no way of knowing the number of illegals that we were missing, nor did we know how many were, in fact, repeaters. Back then, that was a huge problem because we didn't have any advanced technology, such as facial recognition and instant fingerprinting, which would have given us an immediate statistical result. We simply didn't have that capability in the '70s.

Yet later, after I'd transferred off the southern border, the Border Patrol did start receiving a lot more resources. Also, another big improvement occurred when the duty station that I'd been assigned to was eventually divided into three different locations. This was when they put in a side station up at Brown Field, added a westside station at Imperial Beach, and kept the Chula Vista station at its original location. Plus, they added horse patrols; and they started using ATVs, too. So with the new helicopters, along with these extra mobility tools, our agents were able to increase their effectiveness by employing a variety of updated surveillance techniques.

Consequently, in the early '80s our guys were finally getting a much-needed infusion of resources in order to help them better perform their jobs. Of course, originally, when the Border Patrol had first been tasked with guarding our borders, back during the agency's inception, our officers had used horses. But then we kind of became the unwanted child of the Immigration Service, and we simply didn't continue to receive the needed funding to pay for the mounted patrols. Needless to say, the horses had worked pretty well, especially in the canyons. So I'm glad they finally brought them back. And to this day, we still have horse patrols. Also, in regards to the agency's choice of aircraft, all of the airplanes were eventually replaced by helicopters.

-5-

Most of the illegal aliens we apprehended were fairly young. I don't remember very many of them being over sixty years old. Mainly, we'd intercept women who were bringing their kids up from Mexico to join their husbands since their husbands had already been in the States for a while.

Plus, back when I worked on the southern border from 1971 to 1977—95% of our apprehensions were Latinos. We rarely saw any other nationalities until the 1990s, when more Asians began trying to cross in from Canada. During my whole time on the Mexican border, I never actually processed any illegal aliens from Europe.

But then in the '90s, even on the southern border, we began getting more undocumented aliens from non-Hispanic countries, who were attempting to cross into the U.S.

Anyway, when Allen Gerhardt was the chief of the Chula Vista station, he used to come down and visit with me almost every day. He was a nice guy. In fact, in late 1976—after I'd decided to leave the Border Patrol and had put in my paperwork to transfer up to the Canadian border as an immigration inspector at the port of entry in Blaine, Washington—the P.A.I.C. at Chula Vista had come to me and told me that my transfer had been approved. He also said, "The chief wants to talk to you."

As you can imagine, I was glad my new orders had sailed through without a hitch. I then walked down the hall and knocked on the chief's door. Gerhart looked up at me from behind his desk and said, "Please come in and sit down for a minute, Eugene."

I stepped inside his office and eased down in a chair.

"I understand you're transferring to an inspector's position up on the northern border."

"Yes, sir."

Gerhardt sighed and said, "Well, let me tell you something. You're not going to like that inspector's job, being inside all the time. I want you to know we're going to be getting a bunch of new supervisor positions and some anti-smuggling agents. Now, I can't promise you anything, but I'm just telling you that it'll probably be worth your while if you don't leave because there are a lot of new opportunities coming our way."

I thought about it for a moment and said, "Well, my kids are all excited about moving up to Washington State. So I appreciate all that you've done for me, sir; but I guess I'll just go on up there and give it a shot and see how I like it."

And that's what I did. I left the southern border. My motivation to transfer to another job was sort of the norm for a seasoned agent such as myself. It was quite common for an officer with seven years of experience on the Mexican border to want to move on and do something else. A lot of guys down there were from big cities, and they wanted to go back to Chicago or L.A. Plus, they wanted to work a regular 8 a.m.-to-4 p.m. dayshift— Monday through Friday.

To be clear, at that time immigration inspectors actually worked in a completely different section of the Immigration Service. Of course, the Border Patrol was also a part of the INS. And back when I first started out as an inspector, it was somewhat amazing to me that all three of my duty-station's supervisors, along with the port director—were ex-Border Patrolmen. Then later, when I transferred to Investigations in Seattle, every investigator, with the exception of one, was an ex-Border Patrol agent. All of the supervisors were ex-Border Patrol agents. The assistant district director was also an ex-Border Patrol director.

And that's why the Border Patrol became sort of the West Point of the Immigration Service. Now regrettably, as had happened with me, many agents would serve three to seven years, working on the Mexican border. They'd then hit the burnout wall and do a transfer. This tended to occur due to the *futility* of the day-in-and-day-out never-ending workload. Indeed, the thing that finally got me was the repeat apprehensions. When we'd check the fingerprint files on an alien, it used to be—once we'd catch a guide the first time—he'd be prosecuted. But that changed. We then had to catch him three times before he'd be prosecuted.

Yet that didn't last for very long. Soon we had to catch a guy six times. So that's when I said, *This is it. I'm outta here.* The futility of apprehending the same person over and over again was really frustrating. The documented statistics clearly showed an influx spike. There was a huge increase in illegal aliens coming across the border. The numbers just exploded. The volume was overwhelming. For me, personally, I simply needed a change; and I was willing to go to Inspections in order to feel better about the work that I was doing.

My last day as a Border Patrol agent at the Chula Vista duty station was on January 3rd, 1977. I went in—turned in my badge and my .357 revolver. It was kind of surreal. I mean, I was excited; but yet, I was also burned out. Of course, I had some misgivings about leaving the Border Patrol and going into Inspections. I felt this way because, in most people's minds at the Immigration Service, Inspections didn't have the same stature as did the Border

Patrol. I also had that same opinion since the immigration inspectors had a different retirement system. They weren't included under the: "Covered Law Enforcement Position." This meant that their retirement system wasn't as good.

So I knew I'd be getting a benefit cut when I retired. But still, I decided to transfer to Inspections because there were so few other positions that were available along the northern border. At that time there weren't that many Border Patrol openings in the State of Washington, which was where I wanted to live.

I was hoping things would eventually work out, and I ignored my misgivings. I tried to be optimistic because a friend of mine—whom I'd worked with in the Border Patrol—had transferred up to Blaine as an immigration inspector; and he'd told me that he really liked it.

It took me a little over a week to get my family moved from Southern California up to Washington State. And even though I was a little nervous, I knew I had a job waiting for me as a GS-9 immigration inspector. The only difference in pay would be a 25% pay adjustment that the Border Patrol paid its officers, which was based upon working an extra two hours a day per our ten-hour shifts.

Consequently, when I transferred up to Inspections, since I wanted to continue making the overtime pay, I had to work a six-day week. So, like most of the other inspectors, I began working six days a week, which I hadn't realized at the time would be required of me if I wanted to maintain my same income. That meant I had to start working 48 hours a week. Of course, when I worked for the Border Patrol, I'd worked a 50-hour week, yet it was only a 5-day week. But to be clear, inspectors could opt out and choose not to work the added day. Yet I needed the extra money to support my family since I had five kids.

So I entered on duty on January 10th, 1977. Our offices were in an old brick building in Blaine, which was later torn down. It was right at the Canadian border, not far from downtown. In addition to that location, we also had responsibility for inspections at the truck crossing, too. Back then, they were just putting up a new building at that location. For travelers coming in from Canada, there were two entry points. There was the Peace Arch port of entry for passenger cars, and there was the truck crossing into Blaine for the 18-wheelers and freight haulers.

In 1977 an immigration inspector might work one day at the truck crossing, where the buses and other large vehicles would pass through. Then the next day the inspector might work at the Peace Arch crossing station. Now, neither of these assignments was that great; but the truck crossing was a bit easier.

We also had inspectors who'd check the trains that were coming and going from Canada.

When I arrived in Blaine, that duty station had three supervisors. They reported to a port director. And all four of those individuals were people who'd come out of the Border Patrol. So instantly, I felt a rapport with some of those guys because of the fact that years before they'd gone through the same training I had. Again, this was an example of the Border Patrol having become a training ground for the rest of the Immigration Service. It also reflected the fact that we all had started our careers on the southern border.

At the time I'd transferred up to the northern border, we had immigration inspectors and customs inspectors. Immigration inspectors were under the Immigration and Naturalization Service (INS), which was part of the Justice Department. Customs inspectors were under U.S. Customs, which was a part of the Treasury Department.

And there was a big difference. The laws governing Customs generated a constant income, and so that agency had a lot more resources. Customs had more manpower and more equipment—which meant that D.C. was allocating a higher level of funding for customs inspectors.

The import duties being paid to Customs generated a regular income for that agency.

Hence, yet again, Immigration was sort of the Justice Department's unwanted child. And the disparity was quite obvious because Customs probably had twice as many inspectors.

For example, to check the cars that were crossing in from Canada, we might have two lanes open at the checkpoint. So we'd rotate and work about thirty minutes in one of the outside booths on the car line; and then an inspector would come inside the building and someone else would take the inspector's place.

Whereas Customs had double the manpower, which meant that their agents didn't have as heavy a workload. The border-entry process was dependent upon an assessment as to what was required for each traveler and/or vehicle that was attempting to enter the U.S. After an initial set of questions were answered, the incoming traffic was either sent to Customs or to Immigration per directing a particular car into the appropriate lane for further processing.

Therein, if someone needed to talk to a Customs agent, they were sent into a secondary lane, which meant they might have to pay a duty if they were bringing a bottle of Canadian liquor into the country. Also, at that time the majority of the people who were coming down from Canada were Canadian citizens, and all they needed in order to enter the U.S. was a valid driver's license. If they didn't have that form of identification or a passport, they weren't allowed into the country.

Now, another difference between Customs and Immigration was—anybody who had traveled into Canada from a foreign country but who wasn't a Canadian citizen—and say this person then wanted to enter the United States as a visitor . . . well, they'd also be sent to secondary, and we'd have to then fill out extra paperwork on them. If we felt they were admissible, we'd write up what was called an I-94 Form.

So, per the heavy traffic at the border, an immigration officer would rotate inside off the car line after thirty minutes. And almost every time one of us would do this, we'd have ten or twelve people waiting for us in the office; and we'd then have to fill out some documents on each of them. Whereas with Customs, they would come in off the car line and not have anyone waiting to be processed since Customs had more officers and less work to perform.

Also, in regards to employee backgrounds, there were a lot of school teachers, during the summertime, who worked at the port of entry. When the kids were out of school, the border traffic would increase and get a good bit heavier. And so that's when they'd hire temporary customs inspectors and temporary immigration inspectors to fill in over the summer break.

A number of these temporary hires would then eventually become full-time inspectors because they realized that they could make more money and have better benefits, working for the federal government. They would apply for a permanent position and become a regular customs inspector. So that's how they got their foot in the door with a part-time appointment and found out they liked the job.

They'd then later transition to a 40-hour-a-week position. When someone came onboard in this way, they didn't have to start out on the southern border and work their way up the seniority ladder. The Treasury Department didn't require customs inspectors to prove themselves on the Mexican border, unlike those of us who'd begun our careers with the Border Patrol. That was another one of the differences between the two agencies.

Yet still, there were a few part-time immigration-inspector positions that were filled each summer, too. Plus, a Border Patrol agent could transfer to Inspections without having to go to another academy for more training; whereas if someone was hired on as an immigration inspector and wanted to transfer to the Border Patrol, they were required to go through the agency's Academy for that specialized training. And since the Border Patrol Academy involved such an intense series of courses, the washout rate was quite high. It was a much tougher skill set to come up to speed on than most of the other agencies required of their new hires.

Anyway—back when I first transferred to Blaine—within two weeks' time I had transitioned into my new job as an immigration inspector fairly easily. I was out on the car line, questioning people who were driving into the U.S. from Canada. A car would pull up, and I'd say, "Can I please see your ID?"

The driver would then show me their driver's license.

I'd then ask them, "Where are you going, and how long do you plan on being in the United States?"

As you can imagine, it'd be car after car; and I'd have to ask the same questions over and over again when I manned an admission lane. We had several booths, and each inspector would put in their thirty minutes on the line before they'd rotate inside. Then after a short while, they'd have to go back outside for another thirty minutes on the line. That's the way it went, day after day.

And such a repetitive six-day-a-week grind soon had me reconsidering my decision to become an inspector. I was also being nagged by the fact that the Border Patrol had a presence in Blaine as well. Yet at that time it was very small. Moreover, the Border Patrol had a station in Bellingham, WA, and another one in Lynden, WA. Also, a lot of those Border Patrol agents had, in fact, been there for quite a long time. Plus, two of my classmates—whom I'd gone through the Academy with and who, at one time, had been stationed down in Texas—well, sometimes they'd stop by and visit with me. Those guys had mobile assignments, so their jobs were a lot different than mine. They would patrol the Canadian border between the ports of entry.

Now, as one might expect, I was very envious because I soon found out that the Border Patrol agents on the northern border really liked their jobs and didn't have as much burnout as our guys did down on the southern border. And this might have been partly due to the fact that there were less than three hundred total agents—between the western border in Blaine, Washington; and the eastern border at the tip of Maine. I think at that time, in the late '70s, the Blaine sector had less than twenty Border Patrol agents.

Yet as strange as it may sound, it wasn't a cakewalk because some of the agents would get bored with the lack of work; and they'd transfer out for a promotion.

As to the types of apprehensions they'd perform on the Canadian border, a tourist might be turned away from a port of entry because he was intoxicated or because he didn't have an ID. Then that same guy would try to sneak across the border, and he'd get caught by the Border Patrol agents.

So, to some extent, it was a completely different style of patrolling. You didn't have the adrenaline rush on the northern border that you had on the southern border. Of course, when our guys who were working the Mexican border found this out, many of them would put in for a transfer. Then each time a job opened up on the northern border, there'd be a flood of applications. Consequently, a lot of officers did the same thing I did. They'd go to Inspections, or they'd go to Investigations. Most of the big cities had investigators. So a lot of the agents became investigators, which was also a Covered Law Enforcement position. But as I've already explained, Inspections wasn't under the same employment criteria, while both

Investigations and agents working for the Border Patrol were.

Anyway, I really didn't enjoy being an inspector. For me, the work was too repetitive. But I still did my job, and I was proud of the fact that I was able to prevent a number of criminals from entering the U.S. Such incidents tended to happen when there was someone in a car who got nervous or acted a bit strange. When I would notice any unusual body language—or if my gut told me that I wasn't being told the truth—I'd refer them inside; and we then had the ability to do a Canadian criminal records check.

Back in 1977, since there were no computers, we did this by phone. We'd call up and ask for a quick file review. The big emphasis at that time was on keeping criminal aliens from entering the U.S., along with finding Canadians with criminal records.

Another important aspect of the work that should be pointed out was the fact that probably 10% of the inspection officers would make 80% of the arrests. And this would happen because those particular guys were exceptionally good at what they did. Whereas a lot of the other officers, who didn't have such high apprehension rates, just didn't have the same intuitiveness to easily pick up on the lies and subterfuge of the criminals. The immigration inspectors who'd previously been Border Patrol agents tended to have much sharper skills in this regard. They were naturally more suspicious and had good noses for the criminals who were attempting to cross the border.

For example, I remember one night when I was working on a Christmas Eve in 1978. A Canadian taxicab had pulled up and stopped in front of my booth. In the back was an older man in his sixties. He said he was coming down to buy Christmas gifts for his grandkids. I asked him a few questions, and my gut told me that something was wrong. So I sent him inside, and then I stepped off the line to go talk to him.

When I walked into the building, a couple of the customs inspectors gave me a hard time. They ribbed me for pulling a grandpa inside on Christmas Eve.

Shrugging my shoulders, I told them, "Something doesn't add up about the guy." I then had a criminal background check run on the name he'd given me. It turned out that the taxicab passenger had a Canadian warrant out on him for fraud. So my gut instinct had been right. And I think that's why if a port director—anywhere along the northern border—had a list of possible employees to choose from in order to pick the best candidate to hire as an immigration inspector, he'd almost always select a Border Patrol agent from the southern border. And this would've been due to the investigative instincts that such officers possessed. The best inspectors I ever worked with had all come out of the Patrol and had transferred up from agent jobs on the southern border.

Nevertheless, because the work was repetitive, I wasn't happy as an inspector. So anything I could do that was different, in order to break up the monotony, was something that interested me. One such side duty presented itself when I would occasionally volunteer to go down to the Bellingham Airport. Sometimes the inspector who was permanently assigned to that location would be off when a plane was due to fly in. That's when I'd take his place. Rotating in to do his job was a nice change of pace for me.

-6-

After I'd been in Blaine for about six months, I came in one day; and Joe, who was the supervising officer in charge on the immigration side and who also was my main boss—he gathered us all together and told us about a temporary job in Seattle, which was where the district office for the Immigration Service was located. That district office oversaw the inspectors who worked the ports of entry in Blaine and in Port Roberts. The top guys—such as the district director, the deputy district director, the assistant district director of investigations—worked in Seattle.

Joe told us that he needed someone to volunteer for thirty days to go down to Seattle to work as an *acting* immigration examiner. He said the job involved filling out a lot of paperwork for people who were applying for benefits and for people who were requesting extensions on pending cases. The officer selected would have to spend a good deal of time doing lengthy interviews with such applicants.

After Joe had explained the job description, he asked if anyone wanted to volunteer.

The room was quiet, and no one raised their hand—except me. I said, "I'll do it." And the reason I volunteered was because I thought that it would give me a chance to learn how the examiners did their jobs.

So Joe sent me to Seattle. Then after I'd been there for about two weeks, the District Director, Mr. Swing, came up to me and said, "Eugene, why don't you have your wife come down from Blaine, and we'll go out to dinner."

Mr. Swing was really gracious. He was a nice guy to work for. Nevertheless, as I've already stated, I'm not the type of person who likes being stuck inside at a desk all the time. Still, doing the interviews with people as an examiner was fairly interesting; and I did learn quite a bit, during the month that I was in Seattle. Yet after thirty days, I was ready to go back up to Blaine.

Then the district supervisor over examinations, who also supervised inspections at the ports of entry—asked to speak to me near the end of my 30-day temporary assignment. He said, "Eugene, have you been to the Journeymen Immigration Inspectors School?" He was referring to a new training program that they'd recently implemented, which included a specialized course for immigration inspectors in order to qualify them to be better inspectors. The school was located in Glynco, Georgia.

I replied, "No, sir. I haven't been through that training."

Then the district supervisor asked me, "Are you interested in signing up for it?"

This was in July of 1977; and I knew if I said I wanted to do that training, then I'd have to go on TDY for two weeks. I paused to think about it because I'd already been in Seattle for close to a month and wanted to get back home to my wife and kids.

While I was standing there, thinking about it, the district supervisor looked me straight in the eye and said, "Look, Eugene. Nobody else in Blaine volunteered to come down here. I've got an opening; and since you stepped up to help us out, I'd like to send you to Inspectors School if you want to go."

Of course, by that point I'd realized that I couldn't tell him: *No, I don't want to do it.* So I nodded my head, thanked him for giving me the opportunity, and told him I was looking forward to going to Glynco.

Then later, when I got back up to Blaine, everybody found out that I was going to Inspectors School. And, to be honest, some of the guys were really pissed off because I was a junior officer. They didn't understand why I had been selected. My initiative when I'd volunteered for the temporary assignment in Seattle wasn't factored into their thinking.

In September of 1977, I went to the Journeymen Inspectors School in Glynco, Georgia. When I got there, I met a couple of the guys whom I'd worked with at the Chula Vista station, and they had also transferred out to other assignments. I think there was about thirty inspectors, from all over the U.S., who'd signed up for the course. Plus, one of my classmates from the Border Patrol Academy was there, too.

So that trip was a nice break for me, and I actually enjoyed learning the stuff that I didn't know. I was on TDY, which was somewhat like being paid an expense account to cover my meals and travel costs. Also, they'd brought in a couple of highly experienced trainers from Washington, D.C. In class I would raise my hand, ask questions, and participate. I thought it was really good training.

When those two weeks ended, I flew back to Blaine and returned to my regular job.

Then sometime in October, after I'd finished working the midnight-to-8 a.m. shift—I had come home and gone to bed. I think I'd been asleep for about two hours, and I got a phone call. It was Joe, my supervisor.

He said, "Eugene, I hate to wake you up. I know you're asleep. This is a superfluous call, and I just wanted to tell you what's going on. Today a wire inquiry came in. The Immigration Service in D.C. now has a joint agreement with Customs. They're opening up a new preflight inspection station in Freeport, down in the Bahamas, on the Grand Bahama Island. They messed up and didn't get the selections made. They're looking for volunteers to go to the Bahamas for a 30-day detail. Eugene, you can volunteer if you want to. Everybody already has—here and in Point Roberts and in Seattle. Of course, we both know you're not going to be selected; but I need to have a *yes* or a *no*."

I said, "Well, yeah, sure. I'd like to do that." So I volunteered and quickly forgot about it.

Then a week or so after Thanksgiving, I'd been out on the line and was finishing up my shift. I was in the hall, talking to a few of the other inspectors. Suddenly, Joe came out of his office, and he had a piece of paper in his hand. He handed it to me and said, "You're going to the Bahamas in January."

My jaw dropped. I said, "I'm going where?" In other words, it'd been so long since I'd volunteered that I'd completely forgotten about it.

Joe smiled at me and nodded his head. "Congratulations, you're going to the Bahamas."

"But you told me I wouldn't get selected for that position."

"Well, you did; and I have no idea why they picked you."

Then several months later I found out that one of the instructors who'd come down from D.C. to teach the course at the Inspectors School in Glynco had selected me. He'd made the final decision. They'd given him a list of names; and he had, for some reason, remembered me. I guess he'd connected my face to the name on the list.

On January 1st I flew to Nassau for my 30-day temporary assignment. I stayed there for three days, before I traveled to Freeport, which was the actual location of the airport that we'd be working out of. At that time there were only a few Pre-Flight Inspection (P.F.I.) offices. They had some up in Canada, which meant that air travelers could clear U.S. Customs before they actually boarded a plane to fly to the United States. Previously, people who were flying into the country would have to deplane in one of the big cities—such as Miami, Denver, or Chicago—and thus be processed through Customs and Immigration at one of those large airports. But if a traveler went through a pre-flight inspection, they could go through Customs and Immigrations at the departing airport in the country where the P.F.I. was located; and our officers would do the inspection before they actually got on the airplane. Of course, if a traveler wasn't eligible to board the plane, the officer would reject them.

The airlines preferred the P.F.I. system because many of their frequent-flier customers wanted this type of immigration processing. So this was going to be the second time that it would be used in the Bahamas per an agreement with the Bahamian government. Nassau already had a P.F.I. facility.

Besides me, there were also four other inspectors who'd flown in from the East Coast. And, as it turned out, I was the junior immigration inspector because I just barely had a year in as a duty officer. Plus, there was a supervisor who'd come over from Miami; and that was all the personnel we needed to get the P.F.I. up and running since we would only be there temporarily until enough permanent employees could be brought onboard.

For the official launch day, there was a big ceremony planned, which included a handful of high-level INS officials. We were also told that the Commissioner of the Immigration Service would give a speech. His name was Leonel Castillo, and he was the first Hispanic to head the INS. President Jimmy Carter had nominated him to that position as a political appointee.

Now, when us five immigration inspectors had first arrived in the Bahamas, Customs was already there. Their offices were fully manned with permanent employees, and all of their rooms were furnished with brand new furniture.

But then when we got over there, we didn't have a stick of furniture. Again, it was as if we were the unwanted child of the INS. We had to make-do with borrowed furniture, which meant we had to scrounge up mismatched chairs and folding tables. Yet luckily, we had the foresight to bring our own individual immigration stamps with us since there weren't any new ones waiting there when we'd arrived on the island. Someone at our home office had dropped the ball; and we had to scramble to quickly pull things together so we could properly do our jobs. We even had to rent a post office box so we could have our mail sent to us.

Now, during all of this chaos, the supervisor came to me and said, "Because the Commissioner is coming, we need to have a phone line set up. He has to have a telephone for important calls from D.C. in case they need to reach him."

Of course, I didn't think getting a phone hooked up would be much of a problem since everybody in Freeport was happy to see that we were opening a new office and since they knew it would increase tourism.

Anyway, after I went to the phone company and put in a request for a new phone line, I was first told that it would take a week for them to string a new line and to get the phone installed. I shook my head, said that was unacceptable, and asked if I could speak to a manager. When he arrived, I explained why it was so important for us to have a phone put in ASAP.

Understanding the urgency—the manager checked with his boss, got it immediately approved, and promised me we'd have a phone within two days.

We got the phone hooked up in time for the opening ceremony. A handful of dignitaries showed up, including the Bahamian ambassador and Leonel Castillo, the Commissioner of the INS. Then right after Mr. Castillo gave his speech, a guy from Customs hurried over to me and said, "We have a problem. The Commissioner has an important call. But on the phone number they keep trying to call him at, someone answers and says, *'Joe's pool hall.'* "

I still chuckle when I remember that Customs officer telling me that. What had happened was, the phone company had forgotten to disconnect the old number from the telephone line they'd given us. That particular line was still being answered by the previous customer who'd had the number. We then had to get the message to Commissioner Castillo, and he was none too happy about that, nor were we.

Anyway, we started our pre-flight inspections, but then the personnel office screwed up again. When they'd announced the openings for the permanent positions, they didn't do it right, for some reason. So instead of staying in the Bahamas for thirty days, I ended up being there for four months. And since the assignment required that we work a variety of flights throughout the week, we had to put in a lot of overtime. Ninety to ninety-five percent of the passengers who were flying to the U.S. from the Bahamas at that time were U.S. citizens; and they'd flown over there to gamble. This meant their processing was more of a Customs issue than an Immigration concern.

So the work we did wasn't really that hard. We rarely had to prevent anyone from boarding a flight. Yet there were two instances that still stand out in my mind. I remember I was doing an inspection one day, and I had a woman who'd showed up from Haiti. She had three suitcases with her. She also had a one-way ticket to Miami and only a hundred dollars in her purse.

Sighing, I shook my head and said, "Lady, you're not going anywhere. You have to have a roundtrip ticket. Without a roundtrip ticket, you could stay in the U.S. and become an immigrant without a visa."

When she heard me say this, she threw a tantrum. She pulled out a voodoo doll, slumped down on her knees, and started rolling around on the floor. She then began sticking straight pins in the voodoo doll. It was pretty strange.

Hurrying over to her, a pair of Bahamian police officers slowly picked her up off the floor, grabbed her bags, and escorted her out of the building. Now, if she did, in fact, put a hex on me—I tell people it must not have worked because nothing bad ever happened to me in the Bahamas.

I'd also like to point out that even though I'd arrived on the island as the junior immigration inspector, I still had seniority over the other four officers whom I was working with since I had six years of service time with the Border Patrol. That meant that I was the senior officer when our supervisor had to suddenly return to Miami per a death in his family. So that's when I filled in as a temporary supervisor for three weeks until management could bring in a replacement.

I remember there was one person in particular who I got to know pretty well in Freeport. He worked for a major farm-implement company in the United States. Each year his employer would bring dozens of equipment dealers over to the Bahamas for a travel tour, and this guy would help set up a variety of activities to entertain the top-earning dealers.

Anyway, it turned out that the guy was a former police officer who'd been wounded in the line of duty and we became friends. Every few weeks we'd go to lunch and talk about our careers in law enforcement.

Now, after I'd been there for about three months, I was up in my hotel room one night; and my phone rang at three o'clock in the morning. It was the ex-cop.

He said, "Eugene, I really need to talk to you. I'm leaving on a flight out of here in two hours. But I have something very important to tell you before I go." He then paused and said, "Don't use the elevator. Come up the stairway. I really need to talk to you."

When I hung up the phone, I couldn't help but wonder what was going on. I got dressed, went upstairs, and knocked on his door.

He quickly opened it; I walked in his room; and that's when he started telling me why he'd called me. He told me the name of a guy who was involved in a major drug smuggling operation. He said he was one of the top guys in the gang.

My friend then went on to explain that this drug guy worked at the airport, and my friend told me that he was scared his life would be in danger if he told anyone else about what he'd found out. This was an organized drug-smuggling operation, and he told me they'd been moving narcotics into the United States by hiding kilos of cocaine in the wheel wells of airplanes. He said, "Eugene, I'm telling you this because I'm outta here. I'm flying back home, and I won't ever be coming back over to the Bahamas." He then gave me all of the information.

I was shocked by what he told me. And once I made it back to my room, I didn't get any sleep.

The next morning—I met with a Customs supervisor and told him what I'd learned since that type of criminal activity was under their jurisdiction, not Immigration's. Then within the hour, I had a meeting with the head of inspections for Customs and told him the info.

The next day, the head of Customs for the Bahamas flew to Miami and passed the particulars on to the DEA.

Nothing happened at the airport while I was there in regards to all of this. But later, after I'd left the Bahamas, I found out that they did bust this criminal organization that had been smuggling so much cocaine from Freeport into the United States.

Now, due to the fact that I'd ended up spending so many months away from my regular job—per having to work that temporary assignment in the Bahamas—well, because I was out of the country for so long, this meant I wasn't getting the job-opening notices which I normally would be if I was back in the States. It was a concern for me since I wanted to transfer out of Inspections, even though I'd only been an inspector for less than a year and a half. One of my friends from the Border Patrol—whom I'd met at the Academy when we were classmates and who was now working in Blaine—was in touch with me in the Bahamas. We'd talk on the phone every few weeks or so, and he'd let me know when a new position was posted.

So my friend called me one day, and he said, "Hey, they have a GS-9 Border Patrol position opening up here. And there's also a criminal investigator's position, which is two grades higher as a GS-11, down in Seattle. That's a plum job."

I decided to put my application in for both positions. At that time my pay grade was a GS-9, and I didn't want to pass up the chance to be promoted to a GS-11.

Then the supervisor that I'd temporarily replaced in the Bahamas returned from Miami, and he asked me if I'd be interested in applying for one of the permanent positions in Freeport, which would soon be opening up. I explained to him that I was ready to be rotated out. We then discussed those two other jobs back in the States that I'd already applied for. He informed me that he was pleased with my job performance in the Bahamas and that he'd put in a strong recommendation for the criminal investigator's position in Seattle.

I flew home and got back to Blaine in June of 1978. I returned to my job as an immigration inspector. Then about two weeks later—my supervisor, Joe, walked up to me and handed me a teletype. He said, "Eugene, congratulations. You've been selected for the GS-11 investigator's job in Seattle. You were picked because you've done such a good job for us, and you have nothing but glowing reviews in your personnel file."

-7-

On July 21st, I left Inspections and transferred to Seattle as a journeyman criminal investigator. Blaine is 110 miles north of Seattle; and because the real estate market had recently taken a dive, I wasn't able to sell our house. School was also starting back up in August, and my wife and I thought it'd be best if we waited before moving our children to a new city.

So my family stayed in Blaine, and I entered on duty with Investigations in Seattle. At that time there were only eight investigators assigned to the Seattle office; and one, a female, was still a trainee. Seven out of the eight investigators were ex-Border Patrol agents, as were both of the supervisors. The A.D.D.I. for Investigations, i.e., the guy who'd selected me for the job, was also an ex-Border Patrol agent, as was the deputy district director. Needless to say, I immediately felt a rapport with those guys; and I think they felt the same rapport with me per my coming onboard as an investigator.

I really liked the job. We would work area control and investigate criminal activity, such as marriage fraud when someone falsely applied for a visa. We'd also do naturalization investigations, where we'd check to see if there was any evidence to refuse such an application. We might also get a tip on a restaurant or on another type of business establishment, and we'd go to the location and check to see if there were any illegals working there. We functioned as detectives, which meant we'd be out of the office about 60% of the time. Of course, I liked the fact that we would work a regular 40-hour-a-week schedule.

I also should point out that there was an interesting immigration issue which I was first introduced to when I became an investigator. It involved the hiring of undocumented workers by certain reforestation operators that needed low-wage tree planters. Investigations officers were the only ones who actually handled those types of cases.

So my new assignment in Seattle was a really good fit for me, careerwise. And though I was now making more money as a GS-11, I still wasn't able to bring my family down to Seattle because I hadn't been able to sell our house in Blaine. I had a friend who lived in Renton, and he had an extra bedroom that he let me stay in. Luckily, I didn't have to drive a long commute each day since the INS building that we worked out of was near the old Kingdome, which was south of downtown. And each weekend, since it was such a short drive up the interstate, I would go home and see my wife and kids.

Now, when I first transferred down to Seattle, a couple of the other investigators in that office were a little peeved at me because I'd come onboard as a GS-11. They felt this way since they'd had to break back to GS-7s in order for them to land that specific job location. This meant they'd then had to climb back up the pay-scale ladder to GS-8s, GS-9s—before finally being promoted to GS-11s. So they were a bit standoffish and thought because I'd come onboard as a GS-11, that I had to figure things out for myself without their help.

Also, Investigations was a completely different type of work than Inspections. The duties weren't at all the same. I was really fortunate that Phil Stewart, a GS-11, took me under his wing and showed me the ropes. He was this big guy from Texas, and he was a very good investigator. He became my partner, and we got along really well because we'd kid back and forth. Phil was a down-to-earth/hard-charging guy. I truly learned a lot working with him.

Back when I started as an investigator, I carried a .357 Smith & Wesson revolver. It was my personal gun, and it was a Model 66 with a 2½ inch barrel. I'd first gotten the revolver when I was detailed to the anti-smuggling unit with the Border Patrol. I would carry it in a shoulder holster while I was a crewman on a helicopter.

Around the time I'd transitioned to Seattle, the Navy had a big presence in the Philippines; and we were getting a lot of marriage fraud. Shady characters would go to a young sailor and tell him they'd give him $500 if he'd marry a Filipino girl. They'd also explain that he didn't actually have to sleep with her. They'd say that she simply wanted him to marry her so when he got back to the States—he could file a petition which stated she was his wife. Then once the petition was approved, the sailor would get another $500; and the girl would end up working in the United States as a prostitute or in a massage parlor.

We'd get a lot of those types of marriage-fraud cases. But the ones that really ticked me off were the cases where a serviceman's foreign wife would get him to falsify records so she could bring her extended family over to the States by using a legal loophole. In other words, a serviceman would have a legitimate marriage, and then his wife would petition to bring her parents over. This meant she had to fill out an Affidavit of Support and pledge that her husband and her would be responsible for supporting her parents in the States. But many times these Affidavits of Support would later be completely ignored by the couple that had filed the paperwork.

For example, I had a case where a pair of parents were from the Philippines. They'd been in the United States for three years; and I think they had to be here for five years as green card holders before becoming citizens. Then when I was doing the investigation, I found out that within six months of their arrival, both of them had somehow gotten on Supplement Social Security Income without having paid a penny into it. They were making quite a bit of money a month per being able to scam the system via an administrative loophole, which was eventually changed.

So I reported it as a negative concern. There was also another such fraud case that I remember which crossed my desk. I had a woman who called me up one day who'd been legitimately married to an Iranian. And from what she told me, it had sounded as though the guy had been a real asshole to her. Anyway, he'd ended up passing away; but his brother was in the country illegally. She told me, "I just found out that my dead husband's brother has paid a woman $500 to marry him. If you look in today's *Seattle Times*, there's a notice of a marriage certificate; and you'll see both of their names. This is a fraudulent marriage."

I said, "Okay, I'll try to get her to come in for an interview."

The widow then called me back the next morning and said, "You're not going to believe this, but the first girl backed out of the marriage. If you check the paper tomorrow, you'll see his name with another girl."

So I called the second girl into the office and did an interview. She immediately broke under questioning. She admitted that she was being paid money to marry the Iranian.

I then called the dead husband's brother into the office. He was sitting in a chair by a phone. I told him I'd talked to the girl who he was paying to marry him.

He said, "Oh, no. There must be some sort of mistake. It's not a fraudulent marriage. Let me call her, and she'll tell you it's all on the up and up."

I said, "Okay, go ahead and call her."

He dialed her number on one of our office phones. The thing was, he didn't notice that I'd picked up on the same line. I was listening in, and I heard him tell her, "Oh, honey. I love you so much."

She replied, "No, it's over. I'm not going to marry you. They've already talked to me, and I've told them I'm not going to do it."

"Oh, but I love you so much."

Yet she still wouldn't budge.

Finally, he looked over at me, shook his head, and set the phone back down in its cradle. That was the end of it.

So this was an example of the type of cases I had to investigate. Compared to a police officer, my work was sort of low key in a way. I didn't have to face life-and-death situations. As an investigator, the only time I actually had to ever pull my weapon was when I had a woman call me up one afternoon. She told me she was involved in an abusive relationship with a guy she was dating.

The first time she called me, she said, "I've been dating this guy from South Yemen, and there's something that doesn't feel right about him. When he was lying in bed asleep, I looked in his wallet. I found another phone number and called it. A woman down in Los Angeles answered it. She told me he'd been living with her, but he'd taken off with her credit cards and a bunch of cash."

As it turned out, this Romeo had done the same thing with five other women. I'd also found out that he'd been picked up and deported once before, but somehow he'd slipped back into the country. The Yemeni's girlfriend then went on to tell me, "I'm supposed to meet him in the lobby of the Four Seasons Hotel at six o'clock this evening. I'll be there, sitting in a yellow dress. If you guys want to get him, that's where he's going to be."

So I got one of the other investigators, Dan Wells, to go with me. We parked our car a block away and walked to the hotel. Inside the lobby, I was sitting by one door; and

Dan was in a chair at another door. I was reading a newspaper, trying not to look out of place.

Suddenly, I spotted the guy. He glanced around the room, looked over at me, then stared straight at Dan. Whipping around, the guy lunged for the door. I said to Dan, "He's going to run."

And that's what the Yemeni did. He dashed outside and took off running right down the middle of Fifth Avenue. I chased after him. Behind me—Dan turned the corner, slipped, and fell. His pistol tumbled across the sidewalk.

Then the Yemeni ran into a parking garage and hid underneath a car. There was a big guy there who was working in the garage as the parking attendant. He'd noticed the Yemeni when he'd seen me chasing him. Wanting to help out, the parking attendant grabbed a baseball bat and pinned the Yemeni under the car.

I drew my weapon, squatted down, and pointed it at the guy. I told him to come out with his hands up.

After he crawled out from under the car, I patted him down. He wasn't armed. Still, he was as belligerent as he could be and started cursing. Then as I was cuffing him, Dan finally caught up with me.

We put the Yemeni in the King County jail. And that was another thing that we did every day. One of our investigators would go to the King County jail and the Pierce County jail to check the arrest records. We were specifically interested in the immigration status of the foreigners.

Anyway, after the Yemeni guy was locked up in jail, we found out he was a real con artist. And every single day we'd get a call from the jail asking us when we were going to get rid of this "belligerent bastard."

Then finally, once the paperwork had cleared through, he was put on an airplane and deported. But because he was such a slippery character, they had sent two immigration-detention officers to accompany him in order to make sure that he was actually returned all the way back to Yemen since the higher-ups knew what he was capable of.

The three of them flew to London, then connected to another flight to get him down to Yemen. At the airport, right after they'd deboarded, the con artist immediately claimed that the two officers had fondled him on the airplane. We then had to go through diplomat channels to get it all straightened out. He was such a sleazy guy.

Now, to clarify some more of the details in regards to my career in the late 1970s, by that point I'd already gone to Investigators School, which had included two weeks of training and which had also been in Glynco, Georgia. Then in April of 1979, I had come back home for the weekend. My kids were still in school, so what my wife and I had decided to do was—since we were still having such a hard time selling our house up near Blaine—we decided to wait until the kids were out of school, then rent out our house. We were planning on buying a house in Seattle because I had the GI Bill to cover the financing.

So I was home on an April weekend with my family. And to fill in a few more of the details, I'd had a brother-in-law who'd rode with me, years before, when I was a Border Patrol agent down in Chula Vista. He'd absolutely loved it. Then he'd gone on to become a Border Patrolman himself and had worked with me for a year in Chula Vista before I'd transferred up to the Canadian border.

My brother-in-law's career path had soon begun to mirror mine, and he'd accepted an inspector's position in Lynden, Washington—which is a port-of-entry crossing from Canada that's 16 miles east of Blaine. Then after he'd moved his family up from California, he had a child who was born with spina bifida. When that happened, he decided to leave Immigration. He already had a job waiting for him in Utah, and he wanted to move over there. But in order to do that, he had to first spend a full year as an inspector, which meant he was a couple of months short of qualifying for the government to pay for his move to the new position in Utah. He would've had to reimburse the government for the cost of his move if he hadn't stayed at his present assignment for at least a year's time.

So what he did was, he went ahead and moved his wife and kids to Utah. At the time he also had a really good friendship with one of the customs inspectors in Lynden, who was a guy named Jerry Ward and who also happened to have been another one of the officers that had transferred out of the Border Patrol. My brother-in-law was going to live with Jerry for a couple of months until he could move to Utah and join his family.

Anyway, I was home for the weekend, and it was about 10 o'clock at night. I had a sore throat, and I'd decided that I wasn't going to go into work the next day, which would've been the 25th of May.

That evening I got a phone call from my brother-in-law. He said, "Gene, do you know what's going on in Lynden? A few minutes ago, I called over there to talk to Jerry, and the supervisor told me Jerry had been shot and killed."

I was shocked when I heard this. So I called the Border Patrol to find out what had happened. I was told Jerry had been killed by a guy who'd driven away and then had bailed out of his car. They were still trying to locate the shooter, and they needed more help. The officer that I was speaking to on the phone said they wanted anyone who was available to come in to assist with the search.

I immediately got in my car and drove to Blaine, where I quickly teamed up with Brian Rockom, who was a special agent for Customs. I only had my pistol with me, and so Brian gave me a .30 caliber carbine. That's when I was told that Jerry Ward had been doing an inspection at the port of entry in Lynden and had been shot by a fugitive named Artie Ray Baker.

Artie Ray Baker had previously murdered an older couple in California. He'd been sentenced to prison but had somehow escaped. He'd then joined a white supremacist group and had gone up to Canada with his girlfriend to buy some property, which the supremacist group intended to use as a training camp in British Columbia.

When Artie Ray Baker and his girlfriend were on their way back from Canada, they were stopped at the border. That night at the checkpoint, there was only one other inspector working in Lynden with Jerry, who was on primary inspection.

Sadly, it was such a shock to lose Jerry Ward because he'd been a great Border Patrolman and was a topnotch inspector, too. He'd also held the national record for shooting .45 automatics.

Anyway, when Artie Ray Baker had pulled his car up to the inspection booth and had been asked a few questions, something hadn't seemed right to Jerry. So he'd referred Baker and his girlfriend into secondary and then had gone inside to do the inspection. At that time, only a few of the immigration inspectors who were manning the outside booths were armed, since many of them—such as the school teachers who were there on seasonal assignments—didn't have the required small-arms training needed to carry a weapon. But Jerry had a carry certification because he'd been a Border Patrol agent, and so he had a pistol on him.

At the inspection counter inside the station, Artie Ray Baker handed Jerry his ID and wallet. Then when Jerry stepped around the corner and fingered through the wallet, he found a second driver's license with Baker's photo on it. But that license had a different name on it and also a different date of birth.

Immediately, Jerry went back to do a thorough search, even though he'd already frisked Baker. The woman who was with him had a purse on her, but Jerry hadn't checked it. And in the brief instant that Jerry had stepped around the corner and was out of the couple's sightline, she'd pulled a .45 automatic out of her purse and had handed to Baker.

Artie Ray Baker shot Jerry Ward in the chest. He then leaned over and shot him again once he'd fallen to the floor.

Ironically, at the same time that all of this was going down, a DEA agent was laying in, looking for a load of marijuana that was supposed to be coming south through the border from Canada. He heard the shots, saw the whole incident transpire; but he didn't have his pistol on him. It was locked in the trunk of his patrol car because he'd just returned from Canada.

Baker and his girlfriend then dashed out of the building, jumped into their car, and sped away.

The DEA agent rushed outside to his car and began chasing after them. He was joined by other federal agents and local P.D. units.

Baker and the girl then bailed out of their car over near Everson by the Nooksack River.

After I'd been filled in on the details, Brian Rockom and I drove to where a perimeter had been set up around Baker's abandoned vehicle. Before we got there, a Border Patrol agent from Bellingham—who was a renowned tracker—had already been brought in to assist with the search.

As it turned out, Baker and the girl had split up soon after they'd ditched their car. She was apprehended two hours later. But Artie Ray Baker, because he was a pretty good outdoorsman, wasn't easy to catch. He would backtrack and throw the searchers off his trail. He was a master at eluding capture. He'd do things like walk into the river, reverse course, and come out of the water, headed in the opposite direction. He'd also inch out onto a long log, drop down in the water, and swim downstream.

I was there at 6:30 the next morning with the Border Patrol tracker when he finally found Baker hiding in a bush.

Someone shouted, "There he is! There he is!"

I was probably no more than 100 feet away from Baker when they arrested him. He still had the .45 automatic on him when he'd surrendered. And he was such an asshole. He flipped us all off—right up until they cuffed his hands behind his back.

I then watched them put him in a patrol car. He was later taken down to Seattle and locked up in the King County jail. The day after Baker was caught, the *Seattle Times* had a front-page picture of me carrying a carbine. I don't know how they got that photo. I hadn't spoken to the press.

Now, what was ironic about the whole tragic situation was the fact that our guys were always going out and doing jail checks. Consequently, I'd been sent to the King County jail two weeks after Artie Ray Baker had been convicted of murder in October of 1979, and that's when I'd talked to a couple of his jailers. I remember a young jailer told me that Baker was, "A smartass arrogant punk. He thinks he knows everything."

Then an older jailer, who was standing next to the young jailer, said, "I'm not so sure about that. Baker is damn sneaky. He watches everything we do."

Now, the weekend after I'd left the jail, someone had smuggled Artie Ray Baker twenty yards of monofilament line and a little metal washer into his cell. Baker had then tied that metal washer to the end of the fishing line and had dropped it out a jail window. He used the line to pull a pistol up to him.

Artie Ray Baker, along with several other prisoners, staged the biggest breakout that's ever been done at the King County jail. One of the escapees was killed, and a King County officer was critically wounded. But luckily, the police were able to quickly corner Baker. To avoid getting shot, he threw up his hands and surrendered.

-8-

In June of 1979—I flew to Glynco, Georgia, for two weeks of training at the Journeyman Investigators School. Afterwards, I returned home and was planning on moving my family down to Seattle. But before we put our house on the market, I had taken my wife and kids on a family vacation.

On July 3rd, while we were at my parents' place in Wyoming, my five-year-old son was hit by a car. He'd been playing in the front yard and had darted across the road to see a neighbor. I'd heard my mother scream when she'd seen the car's outside mirror bash into the side of my son's head. My father then rushed to pick my son up off the road. It looked like my son's head had been split open like a dropped watermelon. He was screaming from the awful pain.

I wrapped my son in a blanket and put him in the back seat of our car with my wife. I then sped away to the hospital. Before I left, I had my dad call a highway patrolman that I knew and ask the officer if he could escort us to Afton, which was thirty miles away and where the hospital was located.

We met up with the highway patrolman, and he turned on his red lights and siren. I followed his patrol car all the way to the Afton hospital.

When we got to the emergency room, the town doctor told me that my son shouldn't even be alive. The doctor wasn't able to get an IV started in my son's arm. But then a Life Flight helicopter was flown in with a much more competent doctor and two nurses, and they took my son to the children's hospital in Salt Lake City.

Back then, my dad had a close friend who owned a small plane; and he offered to fly my wife and I to the hospital. We arrived an hour after the helicopter.

The whole time we were in the waiting room we were on pins and needles. It was really gut-wrenching because my son was in surgery for eight hours. Then finally, the head surgeon walked into the room and told us the operation had been a success. And that was such a relief to hear. We'd been worried sick that our son wouldn't make it. I later found out that the Hansen Siamese twins had been separated by that very same doctor only a couple of months beforehand—which, as I understand it, had been quite a complicated medical procedure.

So due to the surgeon's expertise with craniotomies, my son's operation had gone very well. A metal plate had been put in his head, and his brain's swelling had quickly subsided. Yet regrettably, he'd lost all of his movement on his right side, and he'd also lost his ability to talk, which meant he had stayed in intensive care for seven days.

But then two days after he was moved to a regular hospital room, that was when I realized he was going to be okay. An orderly had put my son in a wheelchair, and I was rolling him down a hallway. When we passed a vending machine, he pointed at the candy bars on the other side of the glass and slowly nodded his head.

That's when I told myself: *He's doing better than I thought he was because he recognizes his favorite candy.* Of course, we had to teach him how to walk again; and we also had to teach him how to talk, too. And because he'd had such acute trauma, the doctor had told us that if we moved my son to a new house in a new neighborhood and then enrolled him in a brand-new school—such a drastic change in his life would be really difficult for him to adjust to.

Unwilling to put him through that, I went to the Immigration Service and asked for a compassionate transfer. I explained why I wanted to resign from my position as a GS-11. I told them I wanted to go back to Blaine but that I didn't want to return to Inspections. I asked to be reassigned to the Border Patrol.

They approved my request, and I busted back to a GS-9. But I was brought on at a higher pay step due to my work as a GS-11. Still, it took a few months for the red tape to clear through. I'd filed the paperwork in August, and a vacancy finally opened up in the fall when a Border Patrol agent that I knew retired two months early because he wanted to help me out, knowing my situation.

Once that vacancy was posted, I was allowed to transfer to the Bellingham office, which was the best of the three Whatcom County stations for me, as it turned out. This happened in November of 1979. I left Investigations and returned to the Border Patrol. I was sad to have to do it because, as an immigration investigator, I'd really been in a good position; and I'd truly liked the work that I was doing. But of a greater concern to me was my son's rehabilitation, which meant I was willing to do what I had to do to help get him the proper medical care that he needed.

And eventually it all worked out for the better. My son now sells real estate in Bellingham. He's married and has two daughters. He had a remarkable recovery and became lefthanded, instead of righthanded.

Then once I was back working as a Border Patrol journeyman along the Canadian border, I actually loved the work that I was doing . . . much more than I had down in California. And this was partly due to the fact that I had started finding reforestation loads—i.e., I was apprehending illegal workers who were being brought in to replant trees—and my coworkers and I were arresting more undocumented aliens than the other two stations in the county put together. So we weren't just focused on the border crossings. We were also working interior enforcement. Our duties included catching the illegal aliens who were being employed as agricultural workers in the Skagit Valley, which is a large farming area that's located in Skagit County and which borders the southern edge of Whatcom County. Plus, we were working the Skagit jail and the Whatcom County jail, too. And since I'd had a good bit of reforestation experience as an investigator in Seattle, this meant I'd become aware that there were illegal workers being brought into the U.S. to plant trees in the Pacific Northwest.

I would also like to point out that the Bellingham Border Patrol station where I worked was not actually located on the border. The city of Bellingham is about 22 miles south of Blaine, Washington, which is a relatively small town that does, in fact, butt up next to the U.S.-Canada border. To clarify, our main responsibility at the Bellingham station was interior enforcement. We would check to make sure that the agricultural workers had legally come into the United States, along with doing transportation enforcement at the airport, bus, and train stations in Bellingham.

The Skagit Valley, due south of us, had a lot of farms; and we worked very closely with the Burlington and Mount Vernon police departments in Skagit County. Those two small towns are about 25 and 30 miles south of Bellingham on Interstate 5. We'd also check their jails. For years, there had been a fair amount of crime in Skagit

County that was being committed by the undocumented aliens who'd illegally crossed the Mexican border. To the best of my knowledge, maybe 10% to 15% of the crime in the county at that time was being perpetrated by the illegal aliens.

Consequently, the Border Patrol agents who were working out of the Bellingham office sort of functioned as backup officers to the other two stations in Whatcom County, which were located right on the Canadian border. If any illegal aliens made it past the checkpoints and into the U.S. and then used public transportation, it was our job to find them. But our work wasn't just limited to Washington State's northern counties, because the Blaine sector was also tasked with immigration coverage of the agricultural workers in all of Western Washington and in Oregon State. This meant that our sector would occasionally run operational details all the way down to the California-Oregon border. We did this because, at that time, the Border Patrol didn't have a station in Oregon, although the Immigration Service did have plainclothes criminal investigators who were working out of a district office in Portland, OR.

Now, when our agents would travel down to Oregon, especially later when we started focusing more of our manhours on reforestation—or even earlier when we'd do what we called "farm-and-ranch checks," which included documentation enforcement of the agricultural fields— then that's when we'd work with the plainclothes investigators out of the Portland district office.

Conversely, we would rarely work with the criminal investigators out of the Seattle office, whereas we'd interface quite closely with the Portland investigators. This was due to the fact that Oregon had such huge agricultural areas that needed to be monitored.

Anyway, in 1980 my fellow agents and I began investigating reforestation contracts in Whatcom County, around the Mount Baker area, and also over in the Port Angeles area, which is about 62 miles southwest of Bellingham on the other side of the Puget Sound. We started making apprehensions, and this was something new for the Blaine sector because things had usually been pretty lax in the winter and spring months in our nearby vicinity since there wasn't much need for farmworkers until the crops could be harvested. But the tree-planting season began in February/March, which meant that our enforcement coverage had to start much earlier in the year.

I remember one night I was working by myself. I'd been given a tip that there were a couple of tree-planting crews that were staying somewhere in Bellingham. The word was that they were working up in the Mount Baker area, which was in the middle part of the county. So I was driving an unmarked vehicle, and I spotted a van that fit the description I'd been given. The van was filled with Hispanic occupants. I then followed it to a house on Alabama Street in Bellingham. I wrote down the address but didn't get out of my vehicle to question anyone.

A couple of days later, after having set up a surveillance on the house, my partner and I stopped the van as it was leaving the driveway. We found nine people who were illegally in the United States on a tree-planting crew.

The following evening, I was again working by myself. I drove by another house on Alabama Street, and I noticed that there were ten guys packing their stuff into another van and getting ready to leave. I called for assistance from the Bellingham P.D., and two units were sent out to back me up.

Just as the tree planters were loading their gear and getting ready to leave, we surrounded the house and blocked the driveway. It turned out that everybody there, except the driver of the van, was in the country illegally. They were all part of a planting crew. We later also found out that the undocumented aliens had been transported up from the southern border. They hadn't crossed in from Canada.

So those two groups of illegal aliens were the very first apprehensions that I was involved with in Bellingham per our new reforestation emphasis. And getting a tip as to where such crews were staying wasn't the norm because the companies that hired the tree planters had contracts with the Forest Service for the Mount Baker area, which meant that only a very few people knew where the crews would be staying. Whereas over on the Olympic Peninsula, around Port Angeles, Washington, that forested expanse was worked by tree-planting contractors which were hired by the private timber companies.

Now, to me, what was so disturbing about the low-wage reforestation was the fact that the guys who got these government contracts—well, they kind of thought it was them and the Forest Service against the Border Patrol or it was them and the timber companies against the Border Patrol. So we realized really quickly that we needed to change that type of thinking.

I also remember another case where I was doing a transportation check at the old Greyhound Bus Station, which at that time was on State Street in downtown Bellingham, before it was moved to where the Amtrak station is now. I was in plainclothes, and I went into the bus station one day and noticed a group of people that were sitting over in a corner, keeping to themselves. It was six adults and five kids. They were speaking a foreign language, but it wasn't Spanish. And, of course, that got my attention.

I approached an older man and flashed my badge. The guy replied in broken English to my questions. Then all of a sudden, per the answers I was hearing, I realized I'd stumbled upon a group of Gypsies. I learned later that they'd entered Eastern Canada and had come clear across the continent to Whatcom County. The group had a bunch of bags with them. To this day, I have no idea how they'd gotten into the U.S. All I know is, they'd somehow been able to cross the border in from Canada somewhere up near Blaine.

Anyway, this group of Gypsies had made it down to the Bellingham bus station. While I was asking the older man some questions, the rest of the group had quickly scurried away. That's when I decided to let the older man go since I knew I wouldn't be able to corral that many people by myself. Instead, I stepped outside and radioed for backup. I wanted a couple of units to come to the bus station and assist me because there were so many of them in their group.

Two other officers showed up about twenty minutes later, and we stayed outside until one of the buses began boarding passengers for its departure. That's when the Gypsies came out of the woodwork. We rounded them up, and it turned out that they were all in the country illegally.

Now, what was really interesting about this group of undocumented aliens was the fact that they had some stolen video cameras and several fur coats that were sitting in plastic bags right next to their luggage. Of course, none of them admitted to owning the fur coats. Then back at our office, when we reviewed a few of the videotapes, we saw that these same people had attended a big gathering of Gypsies. They were dancing around a campfire and singing songs.

So we processed the whole group and had a transportation van come to pick them up in order to drive them down to Seattle. And just as they were leaving, I suddenly noticed that the two staplers, which had been on the processing desk where the gypsy kids had been questioned—were missing.

Another officer and I then went outside to the van before it left. We found the two staplers and a couple of our ashtrays in the kids' pockets, along with a handful of pens and pencils. Those kids were really sneaky. I had never seen young children steal such things as that before.

Also, since the Gypsies had told us that a lot of the bagged stuff, which we'd found sitting next to their luggage, wasn't theirs—well, those items were then turned over to the Bellingham Police Department. So that was a day I'll never forget since I'd never apprehended a group of Gypsies before. I'm not a hundred percent certain, but I suspect all of them were eventually deported back to Europe.

I also remember another day when I was working by myself at the Bellingham bus station. There was a guy there who had a dark complexion and a heavy accent. He seemed to have only recently arrived in the country. I walked up to him and started a conversation. He was polite. I then showed him my badge, told him I was with the Border Patrol, and asked him where he was from.

Immediately, his whole demeanor changed. In front of everybody, he raised his voice and said, "Why are you talking to me? You're just talking to me 'cause I have dark skin. Why don't you go talk to that lady over there?"

I said, "I may talk to her once I finish speaking with you. But right now, I'm talking to you."

"Well, I don't think you have the right to talk to me." He then raised his voice again and said, "Hey, everybody!

This guy is discriminating against me. He's talking to me, and I don't want to talk to him."

Unfazed by his outburst, I stared him straight in the eye and said, "Sir, I need your name."

The guy shook his head.

I said, "Alright, then let's go outside."

"No, I have a green card. I'm here legally."

"Okay, then I need you to show me your green card."

Again, he quickly shook his head. "I can't show it to you 'cause I don't have it on me."

"Sir, on the back of your card it says you're required to have it with you at all times. Let's go outside, and I'll explain your rights to you." I then walked him out of the building and put him in my patrol car. I next had him give me his name. This was before cell phones—and since I didn't have a radio with me that day—that meant I had to use a payphone to call the info into our dispatcher to run his name through our records. I then hung up and waited for a call back.

Ten minutes later, I heard the phone ring. The dispatcher told me, "Yeah, you've got a keeper. He's an abscondee. He was ordered deported on the East Coast, and he was supposed to have left the country."

After I got the information, I went back to the patrol car to talk to the guy. I opened the door, and his demeanor was completely different. He was just as nice as he could be. He said, "Well, sir. What did you find out?"

I said, "Now you're calling me *sir*. Your tone really has changed."

"Yes, sir. That was just an act inside the bus station." He then tried to bluff his way through my questioning. Yet he'd made a mistake when he'd first said he had a green card but didn't have it on him. So needless to say, I took him in to be processed and sent back to his home country, which I think was somewhere in Africa.

I also remember another case from the 1980s. We had a Saudi Arabian student who was enrolled at Western Washington University, which is located inside the city limits. This foreign student had gotten into trouble, and the Bellingham P.D. had arrested the guy and had turned him over to us.

We took him into custody and were just getting ready to put him in the transport van down to Seattle with the intention of sending him back to Saudi Arabia. But right as we were finishing his paperwork, a friend of his showed up at our office. The friend had brought a suitcase of the student's personal belongings and wanted to give it to him.

I told the friend that the Saudi could take the suitcase with him, but I didn't look inside it because the van was getting ready to leave. I knew when they processed him down in Seattle that they would inventory everything in the suitcase, which was the standard procedure with such luggage. So we sent him off to Seattle.

The next morning I got a phone call. A Seattle detention officer asked me if I'd checked the guy's suitcase. I said, "No, a friend of his brought it in right as the van was leaving."

The officer then told me, "Well, I thought you might like to know that there was fifteen thousand dollars in the guy's suitcase. It was all in one-hundred-dollar bills."

As you can imagine, that was a big shocker. The Saudi college student might have messed up and broken some rules, but he certainly wasn't poor, that was for sure.

Anyway, I was learning the ropes in Bellingham. I should also point out that in 1980, we were dealing with the massive Mariel boatlift of refugees out of Cuba, which had begun in April of that year and had lasted until October. This occurred when Castro said he wouldn't stop Cubans from leaving the island. He then emptied his prisons and mental institutions. Refugees were flooding into Florida, and some of them were taken to Fort Chaffee in Arkansas. Others were taken to different military bases. A group of them was also sent to Fort McCoy, Wisconsin.

When I was picking up some supplies at the Blaine station in September of 1980, I spoke to Agent Keith Miller, who was a friend of mine. Keith told me he'd just been given a new temporary assignment. He said, "I've got to leave next week and go to Fort McCoy."

We joked about it, and I said, "Well, have fun." Then when I got back to the Bellingham office, which was about thirty minutes later, I got a phone call from the chief. He said, "I'm sending you to Fort McCoy. You'll have to leave tomorrow. They need another half-dozen guys over there to help out with the Cuban refugees."

So ironically, after having joked around with Keith, I ended up getting to Wisconsin before he did. And I will always remember the day I arrived at Fort McCoy. There was a protest march going on. The Cubans were protesting because they'd been moved from one place to another place to another place. One of the protestors had a sign that read: "I don't know where I'm going, but I'm on my way."

Indeed, there was a lot of dissatisfaction with the way they were being treated. They'd been cramped up inside the buildings of an old Army barracks on the base. To manage the situation, we had several categories of refugees who were segregated from each other, and we had no way of knowing which of them had criminal records.

Still, we were able to find a few of them who did, in fact, have criminal records. We gave those refugees some special privileges in order to get them to point out the really bad guys to us. Also, a lot of the criminal aliens were easy to identify because of the tattoos inside their mouths. For some reason, certain Cuban criminals had a history of putting small tattoos on the inside of their lips.

Then in order to protect the law-abiding family groups from the bad guys, we divided the refugees into various categories. We housed the general populace in the old Army barracks. The refugees who were absolutely insane, those people were securely locked up. The ones who were suspected of being hardened criminals—they were restricted to another area. And the ones who appeared to be borderline, i.e., the ones who were defiant and belligerent—such people were put in a separate area all by themselves.

There was also a grassy field where we'd set up rows of tents with cots inside them. But some of the people who were assigned to that designated area ended up burning down their tents. And even though we had officers that were watching them from four separate watchtowers, a few of the really bad apples were still able to do such things as start fires.

I remember we had one particular refugee who was a real troublemaker. He always wore his baseball cap backwards on his head. He also was missing some teeth. This guy was kind of an instigator and tried to get people riled up.

One night, he and two other detainees dug underneath a fence and escaped. I was in a patrol car by myself, working the perimeter on the late shift. A few hours later, I was told that a hotel clerk in Tomah, Wisconsin, had called in a tip about seeing some suspicious characters.

I drove over to Tomah, got out of my patrol car, and walked inside the hotel's lobby. The check-in counter was to the left, and there was a restaurant off to the right. I was in uniform, and I walked up to the check-in counter and asked the clerk if she'd seen any Hispanic guys. She pointed across the room at the entrance to the restaurant and said, "You mean, those guys?"

I hadn't looked to my right when I'd walked into the lobby, and the three Cubans were sitting over there on a bench. They'd broken into a house a few hours before. No one had been home, and they'd stolen some money. They'd then come into the hotel to buy some food.

When the three of them saw me, I didn't have a chance to go back outside and wait for backup. So I walked across the lobby and said, "*Hola.*"

"*¿Cómo está?*"

I explained who I was in Spanish, and two of the detainees were very cooperative. "*No problemo, Señor.*" Those two agreed to come back with me to Fort McCoy. But the third guy—who was the instigator and who was wearing his baseball cap on backwards—all of a sudden jumped up and dashed into the restaurant's kitchen. He then quickly reached up above a counter and grabbed a big butcher knife. He next walked out into the middle of the dining room where people were eating breakfast.

The guy started flicking the knife at me. It was over a foot long with a really sharp blade. He was goading me. He said, "Come and get me! Come on! Come and get me!"

Sitting at a table near the entrance of the restaurant, a couple of U.S. Marshals abruptly stood up and identified themselves. I asked them to keep an eye on the other two Cubans.

While this was going on, the dining room was totally quiet; and everyone was staring at the guy with the knife. I was thinking I might have to shoot the guy. But still, I didn't draw my pistol since I knew it'd just make things worse. Also, every time the guy moved from spot to spot, he had people sitting behind him. He'd laugh and brandish the butcher knife as he shuffled around the room between the tables.

Finally, an idea popped in my head. I told the Marshals to, "Send one of those other guys over here."

The Marshals quickly did as I asked, and the other Cuban then walked over to where I was standing. Speaking to him in Spanish, I said: "Listen to me. I don't want to kill your friend. But I will kill him if I have to. I want you to talk to him and tell him to give up that knife."

The other Cuban nodded his head, walked over to the guy with the knife, and got right in his face. He started talking really fast with his hands. Then all of a sudden, the Cuban I'd sent over to talk to the agitator—hit the guy's wrist with the side of his hand, and the knife flew up in the air, and the fast-talker grabbed it.

He then turned around, walked back over to me, and handed me the butcher knife. "Here's the knife, *Señor.*"

Thankfully, the situation was over with as quickly as it had started. And many times I've thought about what had happened that day and have compared it to when such a confrontation would end badly with a shooting. But this had turned out to be an example of how effective a de-escalating alternative could be employed to avoid someone getting killed.

So once the bad guy had been disarmed, I then turned and walked him out of the building; and people started clapping. When we were outside, one of the U.S. Marshals offered to search him. But the Cuban shook his head and told him, "No, no. Not you." He pointed at me and said, "He can search me." For some reason the guy seemed to trust me more than the Marshal.

I proceeded to search him and found a Phillips screwdriver in the crack of his back. He'd honed its tip down like an icepick. Needless to say, I was proud of the fact that no one had gotten hurt that day.

I also remember another significant incident that had happened at Fort McCoy. I was working patrol and had a partner with me. He was a Border Patrol agent named Carl

Greene. He'd served in Vietnam and was a decorated Marine. Carl was a really good guy.

One day we got a call about a homicide. A woman, who'd sponsored one of the young Cuban refugees, had been killed in Tomah. There also was a report that a couple of refugees had escaped and had possibly committed the murder.

Carl and I were close to the woman's house, and we immediately drove over there. The lady who'd been murdered had been in her early forties, and she'd sponsored the 18-year-old Cuban in order to help him out.

When we got to her house, the young Cuban said that during the night—three other Cubans had showed up at the lady's house. He said they'd robbed both of them, knifed her, and stolen her car. The 18-year-old had several knife wounds on him. The daughter of the victim was also there, and she'd given the young Cuban a hug. She was quite upset.

The local authorities quickly put out an all-points bulletin on the lady's stolen car. Then once Carl and I were back in our patrol vehicle, I told him what I thought. I said, "Something about this doesn't add up. I didn't see a single wound on that young man that couldn't have been self-inflicted.

As we started down the road, I said, "Let's look around here." I told Carl that we should spend some time checking out the surrounding vicinity. Then after we'd pulled away from the murdered lady's house, he pointed out another road that went off to the left; and we drove down it. At the end of the road, there was a little park with a lake. The lady's car was sitting next to the edge of the water. The car was within walking distance of her house.

We turned around and went back to where she lived. Four police officers were there, and I quietly pulled one of them off to the side. I told him we'd just found her car and that it was less than half a mile away. I told the officer, "If you take a close look at the young Cuban, every one of his wounds is superficial. I think you've got your murder suspect right here."

Then soon after that, within an hour or two—up in the house's attic they found bloody sheets and the murder weapon. It seemed what had happened was, the lady had sponsored the 18-year-old Cuban; and she'd given him a curfew. She was strict about him not going out past 8 o'clock at night. Upset, the young man had gotten into an argument with her, and he'd murdered her.

Now, I've thought about this incident many times since then. And I think it points out a flaw in our present immigration policy. Specifically, when a large number of people suddenly flood into this country, we cannot properly vet all of them during such a mass migration. This was the problem we faced with the Cuban refugees since there were so many of them. We had absolutely no way of checking their criminal records, nor did we have any idea as to whom they actually were. In other words, because there are certain countries in the world that are unwilling to share vital information with us, then we have no way to vet the immigrants from those particular countries.

So from my many years of experience with immigration issues, per having to deal with hundreds and hundreds of such cases, I really am opposed to allowing unvetted individuals into our country. There's a high risk that a dangerous criminal element will manipulate our refugee system to their advantage and thus harm our own citizens, as clearly happened to the lady who'd sponsored the young Cuban.

Consequently, my 30-day assignment at Fort McCoy reinforced my thinking in this regard.

At the end of September, I returned to Bellingham. Then five months later, in February of 1981, the situation with the Cuban refugees changed. By that point our medical personnel had identified a lot of the mental cases, and they'd been sent to St. Elizabeths Hospital in Washington, D.C. When I was told this, I wasn't at all surprised to learn that there'd been a whole section of Cubans who'd been incarcerated at that psychiatric hospital. Yet I was somewhat taken aback when I'd been told that they were being guarded by a private security company.

And my skepticism as to the safety of such an arrangement was soon confirmed. One day the Cubans rioted, and all of the security guards took off. The administrators then had to send in a tactical team to retake the wards. That's when a group of Border Patrol agents was detailed to the hospital. I was sent there for 30 days, along with the patrol agent in charge of the Blaine station. His name was Tom Gray.

We worked from 11 p.m. to 7 a.m., which was a good shift for that type of duty. At such a time of night, most of the patients had been shot full of Thorazine and had been put to sleep. So we really didn't have too many problems with the Cubans when I was there. And, of course, we'd been sent to the hospital as guards because of our ability to speak Spanish.

I'd also like to point out that a lot of those mental patients were held in custody for many years. Then finally, some of them were sent back to Cuba, although that only involved a very few of them. The rest of the Mariel boatlift refugees, which probably included close to 125,000 Cubans, were eventually integrated into the U.S.

Once my assignment had ended in D.C., I came back to Bellingham. That's when we resumed running two or three 10-day details of agricultural checks down in Oregon each year. We focused on the area around the Hood River, where a lot of fruit was being grown. And the growers absolutely hated us. We'd have frequent confrontations. At that time there was an open-field policy. That meant we could go into any open field to apprehend the illegal aliens who might be employed as farmworkers. Then in 1986 a new law was passed which stated that we had to have a search warrant to go into an open field. So, as one might expect, that restricted us from doing our work. That 1986 law was part of the Immigration Reform and Control Act, which was commonly called IRCA.

But up until 1986, we'd never needed a search warrant to go onto a farmer's field. And so that new restriction really crippled our operation.

I'd also like to point out that I had known about IRCA before it had actually been passed by Congress. In the summer of 1986, Congressman Al Swift had contacted our chief patrol agent and had requested a meeting with him at the Congressman's office in downtown Bellingham. Congressman Swift said he wanted to discuss why several Border Patrol agents had been disciplined for some misguided actions which they'd done while on duty. He also explained that the agents who'd been involved in the infractions had communicated their concerns to the Congressman.

The chief patrol agent agreed to meet with Congressman Swift, and he asked me and another patrol agent in charge to accompany him to the meeting.

At the meeting we discussed what the disciplined agents had done wrong, and the chief explained why he'd taken the action that he had. The meeting went well. Congressman Swift had asked a number of questions, and he'd listened closely to what was said.

After we finished our discussion, the Congressman then asked if there were any other issues that we wanted to talk to him about. Now coincidentally, at that particular time, the IRCA legislation was *pending* in Congress, and it involved several immigration concerns which I had very strong feelings about. I knew if the law was enacted as it was initially written, that it would have made it a crime for employers to knowingly hire illegal aliens. An early draft of the law would also have made it mandatory for all employers to actually verify the identifying paperwork that an employee would be required to show upon being hired to perform a job. Plus, I knew that Congressman Swift had previously voted "no" in regards to this type of legislation before.

So when the Congressman had asked if there were any other issues we wanted to discuss with him, I immediately straightened up and said, "Yes, sir. There is." I then asked him why he'd always voted against immigration legislation that would penalize employers for hiring undocumented workers.

He took a moment to think about the question, then he said that he had to look out for the farmers in Whatcom and Skagit counties.

I responded by pointing out several examples where the illegal workers employed in agriculture-and-reforestation jobs were being taken advantage of by their low-wage employers and that some of those jobs were ones that U.S. citizens wanted to be hired to do. At that time I felt the new law would be very effective in preventing the hiring of illegal aliens.

Congressman Swift listened to what I had to say about the situation and thanked me for telling him what I thought.

Then after we'd left his office and had gotten back in our patrol car, the chief patrol agent proceeded to chew me out. He was mad at me for saying what I'd said. He told me that I should never ask a member of Congress a question without first discussing it with him first. I was surprised at how angry the chief patrol agent was at what I'd done.

About two weeks later, I was driving through Bellingham when the dispatcher called me on the radio and told me to return to the office because the chief wanted to talk to me on the phone.

So I drove back to my office and waited for his call. A few minutes later, the phone rang. It was the chief. He said he'd received a call from Congressman Swift, and the Congressman had told him to tell me that he'd just voted "yes" on the Immigration Bill. He also told the chief to tell me that one person could, in fact, change a Congressman's mind and that I was that person. He said my feedback had actually done that.

Needless to say, I was glad Congressman Swift had listened to my opinion. And it felt good that he'd taken the time to call the chief and tell him he'd changed his mind on passing the new legislation. That bit of political maneuvering made a big impression on me, and I never forgot it. But regrettably, by the time IRCA had actually been passed by Congress, it had been rewritten and the changes which I'd advocated for had not been enacted.

Anyway, back in 1981—before all of that had transpired with Congressman Swift and five years before the revised IRCA law had actually been passed—I remember the first operational detail that we'd gone on down near the Hood River in Oregon. I was with another agent, and we were driving along a small farming road. There was a tractor coming the other way towards our patrol car. It was pulling an insecticide sprayer which farmers used to spray their fields with.

Just as we pulled up to the guy who was driving the tractor, the sprayer suddenly came on and it completely covered our car with insecticide as we drove by it. The agent I was with quickly spun the patrol car around, and we stopped the farmer who was driving the tractor. He said, "Oh, I'm sorry, officers. I didn't mean to spray your car."

That was the way a lot of the farmers treated us. Sometimes they'd even try to block our vehicles from entering or leaving a field. The farmers absolutely hated us because 99% of the field laborers which they were hiring were in the United States illegally. And the big problem we faced in this regard was the fact that we had limited resources, which meant we were only able to go down to Oregon a few times each year.

Still, when we'd run an operation and apprehend the undocumented aliens, we'd do so with a compassionate concern for the farmworkers' welfare. We always got them paid after we took them into custody. We wanted them to get their money and their belongings. We thought they needed to be paid for their work, even though they were being arrested.

But each year the situation continued to deteriorate, and it eventually got pretty bad because there were so many load vehicles—i.e., pickup trucks and vans—coming up Highway 97 out of California. And it was made even worse by the fact that a lot of Oregon fruit farmers really resented the Border Patrol. I remember learning about one instance in particular, before I'd gone down there on an operational detail, that involved a B.P. supervisor in a sedan. He was going five miles per hour over the speed limit, and a local cop had pulled him over and given him a ticket. That was the type of harassment we would sometimes encounter during that period of time, although such a reaction from another law enforcement officer was a bit of a rarity.

Then after 1986, due to the new IRCA law, we faced yet another hardship when it became difficult for us to get a search warrant on a particular farming field, even though we could show *probable cause* to a judge because we had evidence of undocumented farmworkers at a specific location. The problem was, the workers would be in one field for part of a day, then they'd work another field for the rest of that day. That meant we'd have to have a different search warrant for each of the farmer's fields the illegals would be employed to work in, although we wouldn't actually know where they'd end up on any particular day. So the new IRCA law made it really impractical for us to attempt that type of onsite roundup.

In regards to the other law enforcement agencies—such as the local police and sheriff departments—they did not make those particular types of immigration arrests. Yet most of the sheriffs and P.D.s which we worked with were, in fact, very cooperative with us. The cop who'd written the speeding ticket was really the exception to the rule. It was the Border Patrol's job to administer the immigration laws; and unless there was a criminal violation, the other law enforcement departments did not get directly involved in the apprehension of illegal aliens.

Now, we later ratcheted up our enforcement in Oregon and began working where Highway 97 crossed Interstate 84 at Biggs Junction. We'd sit back, watch for load vehicles, and do vehicle stops. Sometimes we'd also have high-speed pursuits.

This type of surveillance would normally involve an unmarked sedan. We'd park it alongside a roadway and scan the passing traffic with a pair of binoculars. When a vehicle caught our attention, we'd do a headcount of how many occupants were sitting inside it. A mile or so up the road, we'd have a marked Border Patrol vehicle pulled off on the shoulder. The agent driving that unit would also do a headcount on the suspicious vehicle. If that officer only saw one person sitting inside it—instead of the ten people who'd been visible when it had passed by the unmarked sedan—then we'd proceed to tail it. We'd next have another unit pull up alongside the vehicle in question and count how many people were now visible in its interior, looking to see if there were people hiding or trying to keep their heads down so as not to be seen. And if that was the case, we considered such responses to be *probable cause* to pull them over.

We'd also drive our unmarked cars through the roadside rest areas. This was a technique we used since we knew that the load vehicles would sometimes stop at such places in order to let the occupants who were riding inside them use the restrooms. When such a large group of individuals would pile out of one vehicle, it got our attention.

Plus, the beauty of this type of investigative tool was— it helped us catch the illegal aliens en route before they actually got to a farm location. That meant we didn't have to get them paid, nor did we have to pick up their belongings. All we had to do was take them out of the load vehicle, get their bags, put them on a bus, and send them back south to their own country.

If my memory serves me correctly, I think my first operational detail, which we called a farm-and-ranch check, was in Oregon in 1981. Of course, at that time the Border Patrol had a number of agents who were working out of the Blaine and Lynden stations; and those officers were permanently assigned to the Canadian border. But since the Bellingham station wasn't located right on the border, our duty focus was somewhat different since it emphasized the enforcement of interior operations, such as the reforestation details over in the foothills of the Olympic Peninsula, along with our work down in Oregon. This meant that we were mainly assigned daylight-hour shifts.

In April of 1981, I went to the Journeyman Border Patrol Agents School for two weeks in Glynco, Georgia.

This training was different than what I'd learned at the Journeyman Criminal Investigators School and the Journeyman Immigration Inspectors School. Indeed, this additional classroom instruction helped sharpen my investigative skills.

Now, besides the Border Patrol agents who were constantly surveilling the Canadian border 24/7, there was yet another type of officer who also worked in the Blaine sector. He was classified as a criminal investigator, which is similar to the position that I'd held down in Seattle. His job description was co-billeted as an anti-smuggling agent, which meant he'd write up the prosecutions and handle the vehicle seizures. In 1982 the officer who'd been assigned the position was going to retire, and so I put in my application to replace him. Then in September of that year, I was notified I'd been selected for the job.

But there was a delay because I had to wait until the next pay period before I could switch over to the new position and enter on duty. That's when I began reviewing all of the paperwork which would be involved in carrying out my duties when I actually took over the job. And even though the transfer meant I'd move up the ladder and again become a GS-11, I realized it wouldn't be a good fit for me since I'd be spending most of my time sitting at a desk and filling out forms. So I decided I didn't want the job and turned it down. I realized I'd be happier staying in Bellingham as a GS-9.

In hindsight, it turned out to be a really good decision. Then in 1983, I got detailed back to San Diego for 30 days. This happened because they had to bring in extra Border Patrolmen since the southern border had gotten completely out of control.

For example, in 1977—the year I'd left Chula Vista— the San Diego sector had made 337,000 apprehensions.

When I was sent back down there in 1983, there were 434,000 apprehensions, which roughly translated to a 28.8% increase in border crossings. That massive flood of illegal immigrants occurred because the word had gotten out south of the border as to the available jobs in the U.S. The undocumented workers knew they could come up to the States and get a job since there was little-to-no enforcement that prevented an illegal alien from being hired. The odds were in their favor that they wouldn't get caught and deported. In their minds, the floodgates had opened; and that's when the huge increase in border crossings had begun to worsen as time went on.

So in 1983 I was detailed to Chula Vista; and almost everyone whom I'd previously worked with had, by then, made supervisor—whereas I was still a journeyman.

I remember working Spring Canyon one night, which was where we used to catch the bandits and where I'd heard women screaming and crying six years before. And even though two extra stations had been added to that sector, the border had gotten so much worse and was overrun with aliens. Robberies, rapes, and murders were still taking place.

Then while I was down in California, a job opened up in Bellingham. Steve Norman, the patrol agent in charge, transferred out in November of 1983 because he'd been selected to be a staff officer at the Border Patrol Academy in Georgia. I had worked for Steve Norman for several years. He was a topnotch person to work for. When they announced the job opening for his position, lots of people put in for it. I applied as well.

On April 15th of 1984, I was promoted to a GS-11 as the patrol agent in charge of the Bellingham station. And that's when I really started concentrating on the reforestation industry. My thinking at the time was fairly straight-forward. I thought we needed to check on the field crews that were working in the Skagit Valley because we had a lot of illegals employed down there. Yet I also felt those farmworkers should be a low priority, compared to the undocumented workers that were planting trees. I thought reforestation needed to be a much higher priority since we only had a limited number of officers.

I had this concern because there'd been such a drastic cutback in the local timber industry. I'd even met with an attorney who represented a group of tree planters that were called the Hoedads. Mostly made up of Vietnam vets, the Hoedads were a bunch of guys who liked to plant trees. But then all of a sudden, they had started getting underbid on their reforestation contracts. The Hoedads were losing 90% of their tree-planting contracts and were being underbid by as much as 60% on what was being charged by their competitors.

What had happened was, the other contractors had found out that they could hire illegals to do the planting jobs. Traditionally, the Hoedads—along with college students and some father-and-son groups—would plant trees in the summertime. That's why I felt those particular jobs should be a higher surveillance priority due to the fact that the work was supposed to be minimum wage and pay $7.50 an hour. Yet many of the illegals were being paid as little as $2.00 per hour. Also, a lot of the unscrupulous reforestation contractors were not actually paying into state labor-and-industry accounts as required. The illegal aliens were being paid cash under the table.

Consequently, that's when I decided to increase our reforestation enforcement out on the Olympic Peninsula. I even set up a meeting with the Forest Service in order to get more information as to how the situation could be turned around.

To improve our effectiveness, I headed a team of five Border Patrol agents; and we went out and hit planting crews. Normally, when we did this, we'd find that 75% of the workers were in the country illegally. Yet this time we came across relatively small crews, and everyone had a green card. I knew almost immediately that we were being compromised. I assumed what had happened was that the Forest Service had summer contract people who were working with them and that they were notifying the undocumented planting crews that we were coming.

Now, from the Forest Service's point of view, this low-cost/cheap-labor arrangement was a big positive since they were getting the work done for a lot less money. Their tree-planting contracts were coming in underbid. So they loved it because the illegal aliens did great work. To the best of my knowledge, there might've been ten or twelve contractors which were actually employing the undocumented illegals at that time in the state of Washington, with about fifteen to twenty tree planters working on each of their crews. Of course, that's just a guesstimate on my part. It could've actually been even more illegals than that since we didn't cover Eastern Washington.

Anyway, that's when I decided to change tactics. I requested some unmarked vehicles. We also began working with the Forest Service's own enforcement officers, who agreed with us that there needed be a crackdown. Their special agents were actually pro Border Patrol. They wanted to help us.

So that's when we began compiling lists of the names of all of the tree-planting contractors. We would know from the casework that we'd previously done before, which companies were using illegal crews. And we'd find out where their crew chiefs would pick up their seedlings in the morning. It also should be pointed out that all of the officers working out of the Bellingham station wanted to go on these details. Usually we'd be up by 4 a.m. We'd go check on a crew and apprehend the undocumented workers as they were picking up their seedlings.

Then later that day, after we'd finished processing the first group of illegals, we might have information about another crew working nearby. That meant we could have to drive 3 or 4 hours, and we'd pick off another crew as they were coming off a planting hill. To handle such large groups of workers, we had detention officers driving a van with us. Sometimes we went out with two vans. For our unmarked cars, we would use seized vehicles. Also, before we went out on such an operation, I'd have to set the logistics up and make arrangements with a jail to ensure that we'd have enough jail space. But we wouldn't tell the jails which area we were coming from. When we'd make motel reservations, we wouldn't explain who we were. We'd say we worked for the J.R. Smith Company.

Hence, we had to be careful what we said because the lawbreakers were really good at avoiding us. They had their own lines of communication and their own networks of tipsters. I remember one morning we'd gone out early and hit a crew down in Oregon at this out-of-the-way spot. We processed twelve guys and then headed four hours farther south. After we stopped and ate, we picked off another crew at five o'clock in the afternoon.

Of course, the contractor who was running that crew was really pissed. He told me, "I can't believe this. I thought you guys were up north of here. How'd you get down here so fast?"

That was the type of cat-and-mouse game we'd find ourselves in when we'd go out and do such enforcement.

I remember one time, a few weeks after we had gotten back from a trip down to Oregon, I got a call from *The Christian Science Monitor*. Someone had told a reporter that the government had one agency that was trying to arrest illegal aliens, while two other federal agencies—the

Bureau of Land Management and the Forest Service—were hiring illegal aliens.

Wanting to clarify the Border Patrol's policy, I explained to the reporter what the truth was, and then the newspaper published an article about it. Soon after that, I got a call from *The MacNeil/Lehrer Report*; and they aired a 9-minute segment on national television of us apprehending illegal aliens out in a field, which was a video that had been shot by a PBS news crew. This was done at a Forest Service tree nursery in Medford, Oregon. We arrested over 20 illegal aliens, and many others got away.

Once that coverage hit the news, it really changed the public's attitude in regards to companies hiring undocumented workers. BLM and the Forest Service began getting adverse publicity. A higher-up from Washington, D.C., was then sent to Oregon to fix the problem. And that's when the Forest Service started sending us copies of all of its reforestation contracts. We found out who the contractors were and where the work was being performed.

Also, since the Forest Service had received so much negative publicity, I knew the private timber companies wouldn't want any additional bad press to tarnish their images. This was because a lot of sawmills were closing down at that time and laying off hundreds of workers. Yet there were contractors still hiring illegal aliens to plant trees, even though the unemployment rate was high in many little towns.

That's when I went to the timber companies in order to explain why they should help us with our surveillance. Out of all of them, the company that was the most cooperative was Weyerhaeuser. Their representative told me, "The first time you catch one of our contractors hiring illegal workers, we'll give that company a warning. Then if it happens a second time, we'll cancel their contract; and that'll be the last one they have with us." And Weyerhaeuser followed through on that commitment. The word got out. The other private companies also cooperated with us.

Another situation that we had to deal with was contractors which would shuffle their planting crews around so as to hide what they were doing. To reiterate—before 1986, there really was no law that prevented a company from hiring illegal aliens. We might hit a crew working on the Olympic Peninsula for one of the Russian contractors; and then after we had picked up his workers and sent them back, we'd be in Oregon ten days later—hitting another crew and finding out that it's the same guys working for the same Russian contractor.

So up until 1986, it was hard for us to get violations to stick. But we also had another enforcement tool because I knew that contractors could be fined for breaking federal and state labor laws. And that's when we requested assistance from the U.S. Department of Labor, the Oregon Bureau of Labor and Industry, and the Washington State Department of Labor and Industries. This tactic actually worked since each of those agencies then began sending a representative with us on our operational details. When they saw a labor infraction, they would write it up. This might involve a housing issue or an underpaid-wage violation. So our coordination with those other government agencies turned out to be really effective.

Then once this coordinated effort began to snowball, the Forest Service changed their tune and became even more helpful. I remember one time I flew down to a meeting at their office in Laguna Niguel, California. Afterwards, they signed off on a regional agreement with the other Forest Service locations to implement a change in their policies.

I'd also like to point out that there was another aspect of the reforestation industry which had really ticked me off. This involved the incredible abuse of the low-paid workers. Over and over again, we'd find the tree planters living under tarps, being paid $2 an hour, and not being properly compensated for their overtime. They'd be camped out up in the hills, and they'd have to pay outrageous prices for their groceries. I remember one time we were over at Forks on the Olympic Peninsula, and we found a guy walking down a sidewalk. He was limping. He had over a hundred stitches in his leg from operating a chainsaw. It turned out he'd never used a chainsaw before and had gotten caught in its spinning blades. To make matters worse, his employer hadn't paid him his back wages; and he'd been taken into town and dumped off. It was despicable. What type of company would do that to one of its employees?

Then a month or so after that incident, I got a call about some Christmas-tree cutters over on the Kitsap Peninsula. The Christmas-tree industry was another group of employers which hired a lot of illegal workers. So this woman called me up and said, "I probably shouldn't be calling you; but I've got a boyfriend; and he's in the country without documentation. I went up to see him yesterday, and you need to go there. They've got half-a-dozen guys who are living in an old trailer. There's no glass in the windows. They've got sheets of plastic covering the openings. It's freezing inside that trailer."

When we went there, it was the only time I ever drove into a place where a group of illegal aliens actually ran towards us instead of running away from us.

The abuses were horrible. This included low wages and terrible living conditions, such as sleeping in the woods and being charged exorbitant prices for food. There was a total disregard for the safety of those workers. It was heartrending. The undocumented immigrants who were living in or around that trailer were hardworking good people. Of course, we had to arrest the majority of them, even though they'd simply come to the U.S. to get a job since they couldn't find employment in their own country.

And to be clear, the reason why so many undocumented aliens were able to get such jobs in the U.S. was because of the way the 1986 IRCA law had been written. Specifically, there were very few consequences, such as fines or jail time, for the employers that were hiring these people. The law only required that an I-9 Form be submitted, which was essentially a useless program. The key to its ineffectiveness was the "knowingly hire" loophole. And this truly was a big loophole because 90% of the paperwork submitted would pass muster, which meant that an employer could claim that he didn't *knowingly* hire an illegal alien. The IRCA law only required that an employer had to *look* at a worker's document, i.e., there was no stipulation that the document had to actually be verified as to its legitimacy. If an illegal alien presented what appeared to be the required paperwork, then that was all that was needed. A document didn't actually have to be vetted, and it could stay in the possession of the worker.

This meant when the Border Patrol would show up and question an employer about the status of ten of his workers, such an employer could honestly claim that, "All of them are legal. They all showed me a driver's license, and they looked like real driver's licenses to me."

In other words, the defining word for the employer was *knowingly* when it came to hiring an illegal alien. But still such employers knew what was actually going on. Of course, they knew. It was obvious. Yet all they had to say, per the way the law had been written, was that they'd been shown one of the required documents. Whereas if the law had been adopted with a stronger verification requirement, then the knockoff forgeries that were being used could've easily been caught. Indeed, it was a glaring loophole. The hiring of illegal workers could've been stopped years ago, if our lawmakers had simply enacted an E-Verify mechanism into the enforcement. If our congressmen had done that, they would've cut off illegal immigration into this country within 30 days because the job magnet would've been taken away. A properly written E-Verify law would've mandated the submittal of documents through a national database, i.e., would've required that such hiring IDs be vetted electronically visà-vis a computer system.

And to this very day, we still don't have an E-Verify requirement for every new employee that's hired, even though such database searches can quickly confirm a worker's status. Congress doesn't have the political will to oppose the cheap-labor lobbyists like the U.S. Chamber of Commerce and the Cato Institute. Our politicians are more worried about being reelected than they are about the enforcement of our immigration policies.

Anyway, as the years ticked by, we continued to work reforestation, doing the best we could under the circumstances. In 1986, I was still the P.A.I.C. at the Bellingham station; and that's when the IRCA law was passed. It gave amnesty to the agricultural workers who could prove they'd been employed as farmworkers for three consecutive years. And in order to do this, the workers simply had to show the corresponding receipts that covered that timeframe. This meant they could then remain in the U.S. for two more years and thus bring their families here once they'd legalized their status. President Reagan signed off on IRCA, and Congressman Charles Schumer was its architect in the House of Representatives.

Also, once IRCA passed, the Border Patrol got a boost in manpower and some additional resources. Needless to say, the added funding was a big plus. Yet there was a negative consequence, too. The politicians were expecting to legalize close to 800,000 people; but, as it turned out, 2.7 million people applied for legalized status. And a huge amount of those applications were, in fact, fraudulent. This occurred because once an illegal alien made a claim, a seal was put on the file, which essentially closed it to further review. It was probably one of the greatest immigration frauds that was ever perpetrated in this country. There wasn't enough time to vet the massive flood of paperwork.

I was detailed to Washington, D.C., when the legislation passed in November of 1986. They'd recently appointed a new chief of the Border Patrol. His name was Hugh Brien. I thought he was a great choice. Hugh was really good because he'd previously been the head of the INS deportation section and he knew all the ins and outs.

So a group of P.A.I.C.s was brought into D.C. by Hugh Brien in order to get their feedback because he felt that they knew what was needed out in the field. And that's why I was temporarily detailed to D.C. We performed logistical assistance as they rolled in new equipment, along with requesting additional manpower assignments. My job was to help the D.C. staff as they implemented the revised operating instructions per the IRCA legislation. I also assisted with the ordering of new patrol vehicles.

Plus, they were able to hire more Border Patrolmen due to the increase in the personnel budget. And another significant administrative issue that occurred was—at that time we had twenty Border Patrol sectors throughout the United States. For example, there was the Blaine sector; the Spokane sector; the Havre, Montana, sector; the Detroit sector—etc. And each of them had a chief (a GS-13) and a deputy chief (a GS-12). Some had assistant chiefs. The P.A.I.C.s were GS-11s.

In D.C. we also had meetings every morning with Hugh Brien and his deputy chief. I think the reason why Hugh was up to speed on the issues was because, years before, he'd started out as a Border Patrol agent and had actually worked on the border himself. He was a real gentleman to work for.

I remember one morning we were in a meeting with Hugh and he said, "We've got a problem. Investigations is asking for a bunch of positions to be transferred over from the Border Patrol." What he was talking about was the fact that when IRCA had passed, the higher-ups had decided that they needed a lot of E.L.R.s—i.e., Employment Labor Relations guys. These employees would go out and do public relations. They'd meet with the growers or go to businesses to explain the I-9 program. This involved the detailed sharing of information that was needed in regards to filling out the actual forms, along with the required verification that was supplemental for the whole process to work. So this was, in fact, the implementation of a completely new education system in order for us to be able to properly enforce the revised immigration law which had just been passed by Congress.

A handful of P.A.I.C.s were in the meeting. We said to Hugh, "All of the Border Patrol sectors, which are situated along the north and south borders, are presently engaged in some interior enforcement. So instead of giving these positions out to Investigations, why don't you create twenty new assistant chief positions? For each of the sectors, you could put in an assistant chief over Employment Labor Relations. Then when the program dies, we won't have lost those positions to Investigations. We'll have maintained our employee count." In other words, we were concerned about losing officers because the E.L.R. program was only going to be funded for one year.

After we said this, the room went quiet for a moment as Hugh jotted something down in his notepad. I then went on to say, "And when the year is over, we'll also gain an assistant chief in each of our sectors."

Nodding his head, Hugh said, "That's a great idea. Let me run it by the boss."

At that time his boss was Alan Nelson, the Commissioner of INS. He was in charge of the Immigration Service, and he'd been appointed by President Reagan. We were at the INS headquarters in D.C., and our parent agency was the Department of Justice.

After Commissioner Nelson had agreed to the E.L.R. assistant chief suggestion, I went back to Bellingham and assumed my regular duties as the P.A.I.C. They then later announced an assistant chief job at Blaine. I put in for it and was selected for the position. I left the Bellingham Border Patrol station and transferred to the sector headquarters as the assistant chief.

-9-

In May of 1987, after I had returned from spending four months at the INS headquarters in D.C., things had drastically changed while I'd been gone. Prior to my departure, we'd been very active in working the agriculture fields. But due to one of the special provisions in the IRCA law that had been passed in 1986, Congress changed the way the agricultural program would be administered.

This meant we would have to handle the illegal farmworkers differently. If an undocumented worker could show they'd worked three consecutive years in the United States in agriculture and had receipts to verify their claim, they would then be allowed to *permanently* remain in the U.S. if they stated to us that they were committed to working in agriculture for another two years. Plus, they'd also be allowed to bring their wives and families to settle in the United States if they adhered to these new rules.

Needless to say, I thought this about-face in our immigration policy was absolutely crazy due to the potential for fraud. I thought the new rules were completely ridiculous. If Congress's intent was to improve the agricultural program, I felt they should've replaced it with a temporary requirement, somewhat similar to the old Bracero Program, where documented farmworkers could easily come and go through our checkpoints without a problem, instead of having to cross the border illegally.

But regrettably, such a revision to our immigration policy wasn't even considered. And it should also be pointed out that the Mexican government had been involved in the administration of the old Bracero Program. Back when it had been in effect, years ago, Mexico's farmworkers were given documentation by their own government officials that legitimately certified the identities of those who wanted to come to the United States to work. Those approved workers had then been assigned prequalified jobs and were allowed to return to their homes in Mexico after they'd finished working in the U.S. I thought that type of formalized framework between our two countries was a better way to properly document who was who and why a worker should be allowed into the United States.

Another aspect of the 1986 IRCA law which really affected us was the fact that we no longer had the right to go into open fields and check people, like in the Skagit Valley. Before the law had been passed, we could quickly go into a blueberry or cauliflower open field and check the farmworkers who were being paid to work those crops. But after the law had been put into effect, we then had to first get a search warrant. And I'm sure the biggest supporters of that change in the law were probably the businessmen who wanted cheap labor.

This meant that instead of going out and rounding up the illegal aliens in the fields, we had to begin taking appointments to process them for the Special Agricultural Workers program, i.e., IRCA's S.A.W. program. Under the new policy, the farmworkers would schedule a time to come to our Border Patrol office in order for us to initiate the necessary paperwork so we could legalize their status.

We'd do an interview and review their documents to qualify them.

Consequently, we found ourselves doing a lot of paperwork. The illegal aliens would show up at our offices with the required receipts and explain when and where they'd been hired to work in the fields. We'd be told the various start dates, how long they'd worked at whatever location, and their rate of pay. It was a good bit of information, and it took us forever to document all of it. Of course, the kicker was, all they had to do was file a claim in order for them to qualify for the S.A.W. program. To reiterate, this turned out to be 2.7 million people. And the fraud was quite blatant because Congress hadn't established a mechanism to investigate any sort of abuse of the system.

Yet the one thing which I was able to do was, I told the officers who were working for me that I wanted to do a personal survey of the farmworkers; and I explained that it wouldn't affect anyone's status in this country. I said, "When we finish processing these people, I want us to go one step further. I want you to tell the farmworker, 'Look, we just processed this paperwork for you. You're stating you are a seasonal agricultural worker. This is going to mean you'll be able to stay in the United States and that you can uproot your family and they can come and stay here as well. Now, this isn't in existence; but if there was another agricultural program—instead of this program— that allowed you to travel to the United States, like the old Bracero Program, where you could come in every year and work and then go back to your family in Mexico . . . which would you prefer? Would you prefer to go through the IRCA process, where you bring your family here; or would you prefer a program where you could work, be paid, and be provided housing . . . and then you go back to your own country at the end of the growing season?"

Eighty percent of the people we processed told us if they'd been given the second alternative, they would've preferred that option. Of course, such a guest-worker program wasn't available to them. Our survey had simply been a what-if hypothetical to help us understand the program that those undocumented farmworkers would've preferred.

And since we'd only done the informal survey at our one office, I couldn't confirm that such a response would've held true with a majority of the S.A.W. applicants on a national level. Yet I suspect that it would have. Such farmworkers simply wanted to temporarily come here as guest workers, not as permanent residents.

Still, a huge number of the illegal aliens committed fraud. If they hadn't have lied about their work history, they would not have qualified for the S.A.W. program. Yet they knew if they were caught submitting false paperwork, that they'd just be sent back to their own country. It wasn't as if they would have to serve a prison sentence.

The bottom line was, we ended up legalizing close to 3 million people. And with a lot of them, we had suspicions when we processed them. We suspected they never had actually worked in agriculture. But they had their so-called receipts. Of course, it's easy to go back and phony up such forgeries. So even though they'd claim they were agricultural workers, they couldn't give us any details as to the work they'd actually done. Our offices had been overwhelmed by a flood of S.A.W. applicants, which meant we really didn't have enough hours in the day to properly vet everyone. We were too pressed for time because we were under a deadline to process all of the paperwork. We also couldn't write anyone up for a fraud investigation since it would have had to go from us to a separate evaluation group, which wasn't available to perform such a task in order to make that determination. Hence, most of the cases weren't even looked at. It was as if we were being told to rubberstamp everyone who applied to the S.A.W. program.

That was a bitter pill for my officers. And as I remember it, the program went on for several years. Yet eventually the policy changed, and we moved on to other concerns.

Anyway, in May of 1987, after I'd been back for about three months from my detail to D.C., I was selected to be the assistant chief. Every sector in the Border Patrol had been given a new assistant chief position after Hugh Brien had proposed the change to Commissioner Nelson. So now my primary responsibility, during my first year as the assistant chief, was to educate the public. And this would involve going to the farm organizations and to any other such groups in order to explain to them how IRCA and the new immigration law would be administered.

Such an educational outreach was needed because one of the other things that the new immigration law did was that it set up what was called the I-9 program, which affected every employer from then on. If a business had new employees come work for it, that employer had to fill out a form that was called an I-9.

And to properly write up this form, the employer was required to visually confirm an identifying document. It could be a birth certificate; it could be a driver's license; it could be a Social Security card; or it could be some other such ID. This meant that every employer had to do I-9s.

But there was also a loophole. The law only required that the employer had to look at the identifying document. They didn't have to call a government agency to actually check on the legitimacy of the ID, nor did they have to verify anything about it. So it could easily be a forgery. And there were thousands and thousands of fake documents.

Therein, this was the paperwork requirement which had been placed on the employers. And part of a new assistant chief's responsibility was to educate the public on these Employment Labor Relations (E.L.R.) changes. So when I became an assistant chief, I spent my first year meeting with employers and teaching them seminars to explain the requirements of the new law.

To help me do this, since I was the only assistant chief at our station and since my jurisdiction covered all of Western Washington and Oregon, I was assigned another Border Patrol agent to assist me. His name was Darryl Essing.

Over a series of months, the two of us met with the Washington Farm Bureau, the Oregon Farm Bureau, the Chambers of Commerce, and the business alliances. We would set up a meeting with anyone who requested information about the new law. It required a lot of travel on our part, and this educational outreach took up most of my time in 1988.

Of course, once the law had been passed, we had more resources available to us. While I was in D.C., I had submitted a proposal for two new Border Patrol stations in our sector in order to improve our manpower coverage. We needed one in Port Angeles, Washington, and another one in Roseburg, Oregon. Port Angeles is a small city located on the Strait of Juan de Fuca. It's across the water from Victoria, Canada. There's a car ferry, called the Black Ball, that runs between the two cities. In 1999 this was the port of entry where the al-Qaeda-trained terrorist, Ahmed Ressam (a.k.a., the Millennium Bomber), entered the U.S.—which I'll explain more about in a later chapter.

Now, besides implementing the E.L.R. mandate in 1988, we were still continuing our enforcement of the reforestation industry on the Olympic Peninsula because there were a lot of timber companies in that part of the state. After I'd put in the request for two new stations, we were given a four-man Border Patrol station in Port Angeles. Then we opened another station down in Roseburg, Oregon, since that area was also part of our responsibility and since we needed a station in central Oregon. And even though the Immigration Service had a district office in Portland, it was located in Northern Oregon and was across the Columbia River from Washington State. That office didn't get involved in the agricultural or reforestation issues. It mainly only dealt with other immigration matters.

Along with the two new Border Patrol stations, we also were given a few more budget items. Previously, we'd only had two anti-smuggling investigators. So one of the new budget items had included the addition of four more anti-smuggling officers, which increased our employee count by three agents and one supervisor. This extra manpower was vital to our border coverage because the smuggling had shot up so dramatically and because we now had human traffickers bringing people in from Canada.

Plus, the additional funding allowed us to have an airplane and a pilot. Most of the sectors on the southern border had aircraft units, and we knew air coverage would help us increase out surveillance ability.

Once we'd acquired the plane, a Border Patrol pilot transferred up from Arizona. He was a superb pilot and a great person. His name was Scott Panchison. He'd served in Vietnam in the Marine Corps and had flown F-4 Phantoms off aircraft carriers.

I think it's also interesting to note that the Border Patrol only hired its own experienced agents as pilots. In Scott's case, he'd resigned from the Marines, had joined the Border Patrol, and had attended the Academy. There were no exceptions made when such a position was filled. All of our pilots were required to go through the same process as our other officers. Everyone had to work at least two years on the ground as a border agent. Then if someone had 1500 flight hours, they could apply to be a pilot.

And such an employment regimen really paid off for us. Our pilots had the skills that were needed to track people. They knew what to look for when they were flying overhead. And because they'd previously worked as team members with the other agents, their boots-on-the-ground experience gave them a sense of camaraderie, which was important. So they really were brothers, and all of the pilots worked well with our other agents.

The first airplane we got was a Husky. By the 1980s, Piper had quit making the Super Cubs because they had insurance issues. A guy named Curtis Pitts had started manufacturing airplanes in Afton, Wyoming—which was where I'd graduated from high school. Pitts' Husky was a metal plane that looked exactly like the Cub.

So the government bought a bunch of the Huskies to use on the border, and the first plane we got was a Christen Husky. It was a tandem-seat like the Super Cub. The Husky was a great little plane with a lot of power. Yet there was one problem with them. The pilots who'd flown the Super Cubs were used to getting down really low and slow near the ground. In a Super Cub, they could circle and then easily pull up without stalling.

But the Huskies had a much heavier engine, and the Border Patrol had two instances where the planes had stalled out. They'd gotten caught in their own propwash and had crashed. One of our pilots had been killed and another had been seriously injured. This had happened because both of the pilots had been used to flying the Super Cubs, which had different flying characteristics than the Huskies, although the two planes looked the same.

And because we'd had these problems, the Border Patrol had ended up selling its Huskies. At the same time that this was happening, after years and years of trying to procure helicopters, we were finally able to acquire some whirlybirds. Yet, as I mentioned before when we'd gotten our first Loach on the southern border, it had been an uphill struggle because all of our pilots had been trained in fixed-wing aircraft. Those guys had claimed that helicopters would be too noisy and wouldn't work for us.

But then, by the mid '80s, we began getting a bunch of Border Patrol applicants who'd been Vietnam helicopter pilots. So this was a big game-changer when these highly-experienced chopper pilots, with all of their flight hours, joined the Border Patrol. Between 1991 to 1997, I think we received 39 military surplus Loach helicopters. And they were legendary because they were nimble and had plenty of power. They were made by Hughes and had jet-fueled turbine engines. Also, many of our pilots out of Vietnam had done low-level flying as overhead scouts, so they could easily cut sign.

Anyway, after the two crashes on the southern border, we replaced our Husky with a Cessna 182. It functioned fairly well for our needs, but we couldn't slow the plane down as much as we could the Husky. Scott, our pilot, would take the Cessna up almost every workday and surveil the Canadian border. He'd look for suspicious cars and activity on both sides. He'd also fly over the farms down in Skagit County to check on the field workers.

And many times, when we'd go down into Oregon, we'd take our plane with us. For an operation, such as a traffic check, it helped to have eyes-in-the-sky.

Scott was a fabulous pilot. When we did our Oregon operations, it really helped us coordinate our guys to have a plane overhead. After 1988, one of the things we did for a number of years, when we'd go to the Hood River and the surrounding area to check the orchards, was to always bring our plane down for the trip. Eventually we also began going to Klamath Falls, Oregon; and we'd base our operation there. It was on Highway 97, which was kind of a main thoroughfare for illegals coming out of California and into Oregon. Plus, we'd go to Dorris, California, too. There was a rest area south of Dorris where we would locate many smuggling loads.

Another thing that was important about Klamath Falls was the fact that it had three different rail lines which crossed through it. We'd go out and check the boxcars, and we'd catch a lot of illegals who were riding on the freight trains. We'd talk to the hobos, and we'd work with the railroad bulls. We'd always bring our own detention officers with us in a transport van.

Up until the 1980s, we weren't actually getting a lot of illegal aliens attempting to cross in from Canada. Mainly, it was Canadians with criminal records who wanted to come to the U.S. and who could not legally enter. At that time we only had about 300 Border Patrol agents—along the whole northern border—between Blaine, Washington, and Maine. There were also times when half of those officers were on details to other locations. But it all changed in the 1990s. So basically, our lax coverage eventually caught up with us.

This occurred because Canada had such weak immigration laws, and the professional smugglers had begun taking advantage of the situation. Therein, due to Canada's liberal Visa Waiver policy, we started seeing travel companies, from Korea and other places, that were acting like they were legitimate tour companies. They would bring people into Canada. This included a lot of East Indians and Koreans. So in the early 1990s, we began to notice a surge in illegal aliens, attempting to come in from

Canada. And that was one of the reasons we'd requested the four-man anti-smuggling unit.

Now, going back to the E.L.R. enforcement, in July of 1987 I'd gotten a call from Jim Buck in Minnesota. He was the Regional Commissioner for the Northern Region. He wanted to know if I'd be willing to take a four-man detail, which would include three officers plus myself, and go to Alaska and do E.L.R. work up there for two weeks. Normally, a special-agent investigator from the Anchorage district office would've been picked for such an assignment. But all of those agents had transferred out, and INS had no one to work E.L.R. duties.

So that July the four of us flew up to Anchorage on a commercial airline. INS had a couple of inspection stations along the border between the United States and Canada. There was also an Immigration Office in Ketchikan, which was in Southeast Alaska. The district office was in Anchorage.

Since they were short personnel, the main thing we did for two weeks was the educational training of the employers. That was the first time we'd had a presence in Alaska. Then later in October, we were sent back to do an enforcement operation with some of the same employers which we'd earlier educated. This involved writing up citations. Again, we were there for two weeks.

If my memory is correct, I think we wrote up 3 citations and arrested 17 illegals. And those 17 illegals came from 7 different countries. At that time, there were a lot of undocumented aliens who were working in Alaska, especially in the fishing and timber industries.

Then from 1987 to 1993, every year for six years, I would take an operational detail with me and go up to Alaska. It was hard work. We'd fly there and work ten straight days, including a weekend. We worked all over Alaska, from Dutch Harbor to Valdez to Fairbanks. We even rode Coast Guard cutters out of Ketchikan and Juneau. One time Darryl Essing and I flew with a Fish & Wildlife agent. We had a report that there were some illegal fishing guides, working out of a fishing camp. We went by floatplane and landed on the Susitna River.

But since the pilot wasn't exactly sure where the fishing camp was, we landed at a place where he knew someone whom he thought might would be able to tell us where the camp's location was. I remember we taxied up to a pier in the Cessna 185, and the pilot got out and talked to a guy who gave him the directions to the exact place where the fishing camp was located.

We then pushed off and bobbed back out into the Susitna River. The current was flowing pretty fast. But the floatplane wouldn't start. We were being pulled along at a really fast clip, headed downstream. For a couple of minutes, it looked a bit dicey until the engine finally kicked over, and we were able to take off. While all of this was happening, the pilot was cursing to himself. "Damned seized airplane! Damned seized airplane!" I never did find out where he'd gotten the plane from.

Anyway, we flew to the fishing camp and arrested four illegals. It was a place which had been bought out by a German company. They had replaced all of the local guides with their own guides from Germany.

Also, I'd like to point out, back when the Soviet Union broke up, we had a period of time when there were a lot of refugees coming in from various countries, which included Russia. But they didn't flood into Alaska. They actually showed up all over the Lower 48. Many flew in legally to the United States and then overstayed their visas. We had a lot of criminals, a lot of Russian gang members come into the country. It was a phenomenon that lasted a number of years.

But most of the illegal aliens we encountered in Alaska in the late '80s and early '90s were from Central America, Mexico, and the East Indies. Many times they had come in as tourists. Then they'd violated their visa status and had gotten jobs. We would apprehend a few of them at the fishing canneries every now and then.

So for six years, until 1993, I headed a detail up to Alaska. We'd go in September, and I went on every one of the trips. And since I was a staff officer—the assistant chief—I had the authority to issue warrants of arrests and set bonds. Normally, depending on the situation, I'd request a bond of two to five thousand dollars. And most of the illegal aliens couldn't afford that amount.

Now, to be clear, the only three staff officers assigned to our sector during that time were the assistant chief, the deputy chief, and the chief. A staff officer had to be onsite in order to properly manage such an out-of-state detail. So that's why I went each time, in order to be able to issue warrants, etc.

Needless to say, one of the best land deals the United States ever made was the Alaska Purchase from Russia. If the Russians still owned all of the land up in Alaska, we'd be in deep trouble, considering the geopolitical world situation as it exists today. At two cents an acre, the Alaska Purchase truly was a bargain. We're lucky Congress had had the foresight to buy the Russian colony and make it our 49th state—which is, in fact, our largest state.

I also remember one year I was sent up to Alaska to do hiring interviews. It was the middle of winter, and snow was three feet deep. The weather was really cold. And I'll never forget that the rental car company upgraded us to another car when we landed at the airport. The clerk standing at the counter told me, "I'm going to give you an Oldsmobile Toronado with front-wheel drive and better traction."

Then later, when we were headed to our hotel, the snow was really coming down. And all of a sudden, out of nowhere, a woman wearing a parka stepped toward the rental car as we were pulling into the parking lot. She walked up to my window and stopped. I had no idea who she was, so I lowered the window.

The woman pulled back the hood that was covering her head. She had several missing teeth. She said, "Are you boys out looking for a good time?"

I shook my head and said, "No, not us." I then pushed the power-window button and rolled it back up. We then went inside to our hotel.

-10-

Back in the 1980s, when we were working the reforestation cases down in Oregon, some of the special agents out of the Portland office asked us to come down a couple of times each year to work with them and the Portland Police Department.

We'd do street sweeps in the city limits and pick up a lot of illegals. We'd also apprehend drug dealers and other types of criminals. The P.P.D. would take the lead on a street sweep. They'd start it off by walking up to people and doing interviews. A lot of the people they encountered only spoke Spanish. And 99% of the ones who only spoke Spanish were here in the country illegally. So we assisted the P.P.D., and we helped get the criminals off the streets. Most were street-level drug dealers.

In early 1988, we had a meeting in Multnomah County, which was a county that encompassed the City of Portland. A guy named John Bunnell was leading a drug task force for the Sheriff's Department. John Bunnell later became famous because he was picked to narrate the TV show *COPS*. But when I first met John, he was overseeing the drug-and-vice department of the Multnomah County Sheriff's Office.

Portland, at that time, had a real problem with drug houses. There was a lot of criminal activity with cocaine and meth. So we went down there and had a meeting with John Bunnell. The thing was, he had this team of officers which he worked closely with, and he'd actually taken that group of guys down to the southern border where the drugs had been smuggled into the country. In Arizona John had met with a handful of our Border Patrol agents, which had included a few of our tactical people, and he'd been impressed by their expertise.

Then later, when we'd gone down and met with him in Oregon, we were asked if we would be interested in assisting John's team with some of the drug raids. They wanted us to get involved in the narcotics busts since many of the drug houses were being run by illegal aliens. John's task force knew we could speak Spanish. Plus, the Sheriff's Department couldn't properly identify a lot of the drug pushers who were in the country illegally due to ID issues. It'd be our job to process those criminals and get them off the streets.

After I'd talked to Bunnell's team—I met with the Deputy District Director, Seth Libby, out of the Portland Immigration Office; and we were given the green light to proceed. Consequently, the coordinated effort between our officers and Bunnell's task force went on for a number of years. I remember the first drug raid we worked in Portland. It involved four separate residences, and the task force took all of the drug houses down at the exact same time. It was a really big haul, and they must've had at least a hundred different officers involved in that huge bust. A variety of agencies from different jurisdictions had been brought in, including agents from the FBI and the DEA— along with county law enforcement officers.

A Border Patrol agent was assigned to each of the houses. Of course, this was back before we had cell phones. The team I was with was in an undercover van, and we'd parked it several blocks away from the house which we were targeting. Throughout the city, they had undercover units watching the other three houses. At the same time, they had officers at the courthouse who were filing the legal paperwork for the probable cause in order to get the search warrants to hit the houses.

I remember we sat in that van for two hours, waiting to hear back from the courthouse. People were farting, and there was a lot of body odor. It wasn't pleasant. We were cramped in there, just hoping we'd get a *go* ASAP.

Then finally, we got a confirmation on our walkie-talkies. We were told that the judge had signed off on the warrants and that we'd execute them in ten minutes. The team leader said, "Everybody saddle up." And immediately, when he said this, everything went quiet. We put on our body armor. I had a short-barrel MP5 semiautomatic 9-millimeter Heckler & Koch that I carried, and I double-checked its safety.

Sitting next to the van's back door was a deputy that was an ex-wrestler. He was holding a steel-plated battering ram, which we called a key, that he'd use to bust in the door. It had handholds welded onto both of its sides.

So the van sped over to the drug house and skidded to a stop at a nearby curb. The next-door neighbor was mowing his lawn. I remember we piled out of that vehicle and crossed right in front of the guy with the lawnmower. We were all in uniform. I was following right behind the officer with the battering ram, who was leading the way. We charged up to the house's front door, and he yelled, "Police!"

BOOM!

The deputy hit that door, and the whole doorframe went down. I was the second officer inside because I could give the commands in Spanish. *"Los manos arriba! Los manos arriba!"*

There were two guys sitting in the living room on a sofa, watching television. They complied and raised their hands. We swarmed in and took them down. They didn't resist. Under the sofa cushion of one of the guys was a loaded .45 auto pistol.

So that was the first drug raid we did. I remember on that bust we got seven illegal aliens and thirty-four pounds of cocaine—which was a record haul. It was the most cocaine the task force had ever confiscated up until that point. We also found a pound of black tar heroin in the house, too, along with twenty-six weapons. Plus, we seized thirteen vehicles and $12,000 in cash.

We later found out that a cartel had been selling drugs out of the house. And over the years, there were probably at least another half-a-dozen drug operations that we did in the 1980s where we went in and assisted other agencies. Of course, once everyone was under arrest, then the real work would begin. We'd have to take them to jail and start processing them. The ones who didn't have any hard charges on them, we'd arrest under immigration charges and deport them—i.e., we'd put them under deportation proceedings.

So that was how we would cooperate with the various police departments. Also, before that first case, I remember back when John Bunnell had stood up in an early planning meeting. He'd told his officers, "I'm happy to tell you that we have seven people here today from the U.S. Border Patrol. And, in my opinion, the Border Patrol is the only organization that the cartels really fear."

But, needless to say, now things have changed. And the irony of it to me is—the Border Patrol doesn't even get cooperation from some of our other law enforcement agencies due to the sanctuary city restrictions and due to the mindset of certain localities that are trying to limit the immigration laws. I think it's criminal for a California mayor to go out in public and tip illegals that ICE is looking for them. We used to work hand in hand with the local police departments. We were partners. As federal law enforcement officers, our job has always been to enforce the law and to protect American citizens from harm.

So because of the present political climate, things have actually regressed. And the sad part is, the majority of crimes that are committed against people who are in this country illegally are actually perpetrated by other undocumented aliens who are, in fact, criminals. So, in my opinion, we still should be working hand in hand with the local police departments to stop crime.

As someone once explained it to me—if a married couple with two small kids owns a home, they don't want a group of strangers camping out in their garage. It's the couple's private property, and they have a right to keep trespassers from invading their home and possibly harming their kids.

Likewise, this is our country, and our government has the right to keep people from coming here illegally. We can't just let anyone who wants to move here proceed to do so without any regard to documenting who they are. We must be able to control our borders. Otherwise, tens of millions of people will be flooding into the U.S., and they will be ignoring our immigration laws.

So to me, asking a homeowner's permission before someone is allowed to camp out in their garage is a perfect analogy. We need to make sure our laws are properly enforced in order to protect our citizens. A homeowner has the right to keep strangers from coming inside his or her house, just as the citizens of this country—via Congress— have the right to control who is or who is not allowed to enter the United States.

And this was one of the things, as a trainee Border Patrol agent, that really irritated me when I'd see so many illegal aliens flooding across the border. *What right did they have to do what they were doing? This is my country. I wanted to ask them why they felt they could simply ignore our laws.*

And to extend out the above analogy, Mexico would not want millions of U.S. citizens to illegally enter Mexico and take jobs away from Mexicans. They wouldn't allow such a thing to happen. Their government officials would do everything they could to stop such an invasion of their sovereignty by non-Mexicans. Yet for some reason, Mexico doesn't want the United States to close its borders and thus restrict who we let in our country.

So, in my opinion, there's a self-serving subjectivity that drives the thinking of those who are advocating for us to open our borders and thus ignore our own immigration laws. This type of political policy only benefits other countries and does not adequately protect the rights of our U.S. citizens.

Of course, as I've clearly stated before, there are many hardworking illegal aliens who have come to the United States to simply get a job. And to the best of my knowledge, less than 10% or so of those migrants ever end up committing a criminal act. Yet the law is the law. And if this is, in fact, a country of laws, then we need to enforce our immigration policies and *require* municipalities to coordinate their local law enforcement officers with our federal officers. That's the bottom line.

I think what's presently happening in our country with the deadly Mexican drug cartels and the South American gangs, such as MS-13—is a huge *red flag*. There was even a series of murders on Long Island where ICE had to assist with the investigation of a dangerous gang of El Salvadorians.

Indeed, it really bothers me how the sanctuary city advocates are manipulating the thinking of the American public. When I look at what's going on in California and read news reports about Jay Inslee, our governor, wanting to declare Washington a sanctuary state, I get very concerned. And a perfect example of why local and federal law enforcement agencies need to communicate with each other on immigration issues is the D.C. sniper case.

In regards to what had happened with that particular mass-murder investigation—there was a Bellingham police officer who'd encountered Lee Malvo's mother (whose name was Una James) on a domestic disturbance complaint. She was trying to get her son—who was seventeen years old at the time—away from John Allen Muhammad because he'd taken Lee Malvo under his wing. Malvo's mother had a bunch of suitcases filled with her belongings, and she was attempting to get her son out of town. So that's when the Bellingham police officer had come in contact with her. He suspected that she could be in the country illegally due of her weak language skills.

To confirm his suspicion, the police officer had called the Border Patrol. Keith Olson—one of my good friends who was an agent at the time—responded to the call. He determined that Malvo's mother was, in fact, an illegal alien. She also told him about her son. Keith then asked her where her son was. She replied that he was at the Lighthouse Mission and that he was with John Allen Muhammad.

Another agent then brought Malvo's mother in for processing, and Keith went to the Lighthouse Mission. But when he got there, he couldn't find Lee Malvo and Muhammad. That's when a guy at the Mission told Keith that the two of them might be at the YMCA because they would sometimes work out there.

So Keith went to the YMCA and checked out the locker room. That's where he found Malvo and Muhammad. Keith walked up to Malvo and started talking to him.

Surprisingly, Malvo nodded his head and admitted that he was in the country illegally and that he was a Jamaican.

Keith Olson then turned and talked to Muhammad. But Muhammad was standoffish, and he sort of distanced himself from the questioning. Keith later told me, when he noticed Muhammad's reaction, that the hairs stood up on the back of his neck.

Yet there was a legal problem because Muhammad was a U.S. citizen. So Keith then called P.D. for backup. But the police couldn't do anything since they couldn't prove that Muhammad had had anything to do with bringing Malvo into the country. That meant Muhammad was not taken into custody.

When the Border Patrol processed Malvo and his mother, she claimed they'd come into the U.S. as stowaways on a ship. That turned out to be a legal loophole because stowaways are categorized as a unique category and cannot be released. Per the law, stowaways have to be taken into custody and returned to the shipping company which brought them into the country, and then that shipping company is required to transport them back to their country of origin.

But later, when Malvo's mother had been moved down to the detention facility in Seattle, she changed her story. She next claimed she'd actually been smuggled into Florida. After Muhammad's record was checked to see if her statement could be substantiated, it turned out that he'd been arrested a few times for various crimes. But it gets even more convoluted because Muhammad had been in the U.S. Army and he'd converted to Islam. That's when he'd changed his name to Muhammad.

Also, as far as I'm aware of, certain aspects of the case were never made public. I happen to know the chief investigator for the House Judiciary Committee. He told me, when he was tasked with researching the D.C. sniper attacks for Congress, that he'd gone to Jamaica and Antigua to nail down as many of the facts as he could. He said that Muhammad had, in fact, been involved in smuggling aliens into the U.S. and that was why he'd been up in the Pacific Northwest. He'd been bringing illegal aliens into Canada from Antigua.

Anyway, not long after Muhammad had been questioned at the YMCA—another shoe dropped. This happened when Malvo was cut loose, and the seventeen-year-old kid quickly hooked back up with Muhammad in Bellingham.

They later drove to Tacoma, Washington, and killed a woman. Shortly thereafter, the two of them went on their cross-country killing spree and murdered a total of 17 people before they were finally caught in Maryland.

There's also another very interesting aspect to the D.C. sniper case. During the time the two of them were traveling around and killing people, Lee Malvo was calling and harassing the FBI. He'd say something like, "Oh, you think you're good? We're bad. We're bad." Then in one of his calls, he mentioned Montgomery, Alabama, which was where they'd killed a liquor-store clerk. But the thing was, at the time the FBI hadn't tied that murder to the D.C. snipings.

It also turned out that a local police officer had almost caught Malvo at that Montgomery crime scene. In his hurry to get away, Malvo had dropped a gun-ad brochure. The brochure had been picked up by the police, but they hadn't checked it for fingerprints until the FBI had later called them about it. So that case had initially been labeled an unsolved murder. Then once the law enforcement officers had connected the dots, they realized the D.C. murders and that killing in Alabama had the same *modus operandi*.

When they ran the prints, Malvo's arrest in Bellingham by the Border Patrol had popped up. Keith Olson's apprehension of the seventeen-year-old illegal alien from Jamaica was key to solving the D.C. sniper attacks. That's how they'd identified the young shooter.

Now, the ironic thing was, I'd already retired from the Border Patrol by then and was working for the National Counterdrug Training Center, where we were training people from different agencies to work together. The Bellingham police officer who'd called the Border Patrol about Malvo's mother had recently been promoted; and he was now the P.D.'s intelligence officer. He was attending a class I was teaching, and he got a phone call. After he hung up, he told me, "I think there's some connection with the D.C. sniper to Bellingham."

I was at first a bit skeptical. But then about thirty minutes later, John Bates—who was the deputy chief and who'd taken over my job after I'd retired—came over to the building I was working in. He pulled me aside and said, "You're not going to believe this, Gene." He then told me the date that Keith Olson had arrested the seventeen-year-old Jamaican here in Bellingham. John said, "Lee Boyd Malvo is one of the D.C. snipers."

And, of course, the reason the FBI was able to solve that mass-murder case was because of the cooperation between a Bellingham Border Patrol agent and a Bellingham police officer. But now, the Bellingham P.D. doesn't cooperate with the Border Patrol anymore because of the attitude of the city council; and that's the real irony of our present-day political climate. Bellingham didn't officially declare itself a "sanctuary city," but it did institute policies to limit the contact between its police officers and the Border Patrol.

Also, after the 9/11 attacks and before Malvo and Muhammad had gone on their killing spree, Keith Olson and I were asked to testify before Senator Carl Levin's Select Committee on Investigations. And one of the things we talked about in that Congressional hearing, when the subject of immigration had come up, was how the 9/11 terrorists had gotten into the country. We discussed why so many people were being apprehended on the border and why they were then being released. I talked about our Border Patrol officers catching illegal aliens and having to cut them loose once they were scheduled for an immigration hearing, with many of them disappearing and not showing up for their court dates.

Then six weeks after the two of us had testified before Congress about having to release many of the undocumented aliens which were being apprehended— that's when Keith had arrested Lee Malvo, and that's when Malvo had later been cut loose once he'd been sent down to Seattle for detention.

To me, that was a very cruel irony, considering the fact that Malvo had been arrested in Bellingham and then had gone on to murder 17 people with John Allen Muhammad. That's why I'm so concerned about the American public being manipulated by pro-immigrant political groups and their constant feel-sorry-for-the-illegal-aliens drumbeat. Still, I do understand the emotional sentiment involved, and I think we should continue to allow *legal* immigration. But I think it's wrong to let known criminals come into our country. I'm for documented immigrants being properly vetted, and they should only be allowed into the U.S. via a legal process.

For example, I remember when I was a GS-9 Border Patrol agent in Bellingham. One of the guys I worked with got a call from a Bellingham police officer who'd arrested a guy for shoplifting.

The agent responded, but I don't recall if the shoplifter had a criminal record in the U.S. or not. The guy might have had some arrests in Canada, although he didn't have any outstanding warrants.

Anyway, the agent took the guy into custody and returned him to Canada. The shoplifter was dropped off at the border, and his name was written up in the apprehension book. A year later, that same guy's name popped back up. His name was Clifford Olson; and over a series of years, he'd killed 11 kids in British Columbia. He was a mass murderer. So Clifford Olson's Border Patrol apprehension had occurred due to a phone call from the Bellingham P.D. and due to the fact that the two agencies could, at that time, coordinate their efforts to enforce our immigration laws and thus protect U.S. citizens from criminal activity.

In my opinion, it's absolutely insane for any local law enforcement agency to be prohibited from sharing information with another law enforcement agency. Such "sanctuary city" thinking makes no sense to me. And that's why I'm hoping this book will open people's eyes. I truly think when our immigration policies are properly explained to the American public, then the voters will have a better understanding as to why we need E-Verify and why such a law hasn't been passed by Congress.

I also think it's a misnomer when people say that there are a lot of jobs that U.S. citizens won't do. I don't believe that is correct. A more accurate assessment would be: There are a lot of jobs that U.S. citizens don't want to do at the low hourly wage that certain employers offer to pay them. And that's a concern since these same employers are now using the H-2 program to bring in agricultural workers, but then we still hear the horrible stories of how the farmworkers are being taken advantage of. They're being crammed into poorly maintained vehicles. The housing they're given is substandard. Sometimes they're not paid for their overtime work, and not all of their employers offer them proper medical care.

So, in one respect, even though we've had some well-meaning politicians over the years who've attempted to do the right thing in regards to our guest-worker policies, the actual implementation of the different programs hasn't been as effective as it should've been.

I'm reminded how angry I got one time. On a trip to see my mother in Utah, shortly after she'd had a stroke, I'd stopped at a rest area near Mountain Home Air Force Base in Idaho. This was a week after I'd come back from teaching a border-control training course in Nigeria. I was driving a Volkswagen van, a Westfalia, which I would sleep in.

So I'd gotten to the rest area at around 11 p.m. It was late, and I was pretty tired. I called it a night.

Then around 7:30 the next morning, I got a call from my daughter. She was in tears. She said, "Dad, are you hearing what's going on in the news?"

I said, "No, I haven't had the radio on. What's wrong?"

She told me about the two planes which had crashed into the World Trade Center in New York City. She was calling me on a Tuesday morning, and it was September 11th, 2001.

Now, having known the threat from the two terrorists cases we'd already worked in Bellingham, along with the intelligence I'd read, I absolutely knew who the 9/11 perpetrators would turn out to be. I knew it was going to be foreigners who'd come into our country—one way or another—and I knew some of them would be illegal aliens, although I also assumed a number of them would, in fact, be here legally. After having previously testified to Congress about what I considered to be the *red flags* that were facing our country, I was upset. I was really furious when my daughter had called me and told me what had happened in New York City.

Then three or four days later, while I was still visiting with my mother in Utah, that's when I started getting a bunch of phone calls. All of a sudden, because of my Congressional testimony, I had a lot of press people calling me. And one of the reporters who called me was Gilbert Gaul. He was a two-time Pulitzer prize-winning journalist from the *Washington Post.*

I said, "Gil, if you want to know how the terrorists got in the country, if you want to know the weaknesses, if you want to know how bad stuff is with immigration complacency . . . Congressman Lamar Smith, the Chairman of the Judiciary Committee on Immigration, has had a series of hearings that have gone on for almost three years. He's identified every one of the weaknesses. And nobody pays attention to him. So I think you need to dig into what he's uncovered. If you do, you'll find a treasure-trove of articles."

The following weekend, the *Washington Post* had a frontpage headline that read: "The INS Can't Track Anybody"—or wording close to that.

Again, I think every country has a right to control its borders and decide who can or who cannot immigrate. When refugees are given permission to enter the U.S., it must be done with full vetting and proper documentation. As I've already stated, most people will not allow a group of complete strangers to simply show up on their doorstep, barge inside their home, and demand to stay there for several years. The analogy is similar to letting illegal aliens come into our country. There must be a vetting process that's adhered to in order to verify people's identities, and there also needs to be a compelling humanitarian reason as to why we should allow such people into the United States.

One only has to remember the mass Cuban migration of 1980, during the Mariel boatlift. What was most disturbing about that situation was the fact that so many criminals had been allowed to come into our country as refugees. They were not vetted, and these were people we should never have let in the United States.

To me, it's absurd that certain politicians are trying to change history. For example, Shelia Jackson Lee seems to have forgotten what was recommended to Congress by its own Commission on Immigration Reform. Ms. Lee is a U.S. Representative from Texas, and she was at the Judiciary Committee on Immigration hearing which I testified at before I retired from the Border Patrol. It's important to note that I'd personally met Barbara Jordan, who was also a U.S. Representative from Texas. Plus, before I was introduced to Barbara Jordan, I'd read the Jordan Report, which included a number of recommendations that her Commission on Immigration Reform had made in 1995 and then had proceeded to issue a final assessment of in 1997.

So when Congresswoman Shelia Jackson Lee states that Barbara Jordan wasn't in favor of E-Verify, I respectfully must dispute those words. Congresswoman Barbara Jordan was, in fact, very much in favor of E-Verify. She also wanted to eliminate chain immigration and thought that we needed to enforce better documentation.

Specially, Barbara Jordan said that our immigration policy should accomplish three primary goals. First, it should allow people into the U.S. who have a legal right to be here. Second, it should stop people from entering our country if they have no lawful right to be here. Third, it should remove people if they're not supposed to be here.

Indeed, I was quite impressed by the Jordan Commission. It was made up of half Democrats and half Republicans. They were bipartisan, and they seemed to genuinely like each other. I think they put together a well-thought-out and comprehensive report on immigration.

But then, due to opposition from many cheap-labor and pro-immigrant groups such as the U.S. Chamber of Commerce and the Cato Institute, the Jordan Commission's recommendations never really got to first base. This involved the self-serving politics of maintaining a system of low-paid workers, which certain businesses had lobbied Congress to keep in place. And regrettably, there never was much press coverage of the harm that was being done to our own citizens per the loss of jobs and per the widespread criminal activities of the undocumented immigrants.

The events of 9/11 are yet another example of the terrible hardships that thousands and thousands of our U.S. citizens had to suffer through due to our flawed immigration policies. The 9/11 terrorists were able to enter our country and perpetrate their crimes because we were not properly vetting the border documentation, nor were our law enforcement agencies proactively communicating with each other.

-11-

I've already explained some of the enforcement issues we faced back when the Blaine sector had been given the two new Border Patrol stations. One station was opened in Port Angeles, Washington; and the other was opened in Roseburg, Oregon. We were also given the anti-smuggling units.

As we then progressed into the 1990s, the increased manpower was a big asset to our effectiveness. But the one thing that was negatively affecting our surveillance abilities was the new IRCA law. There was a massive amount of document fraud, and this was taking a lot of our time to review. Still, the increased paperwork wasn't slowing down our apprehensions.

For example, at our Roseburg station, a Border Patrol agent one day responded to a call from the Oregon State Police. They'd done a vehicle stop, and there were four undocumented aliens in the car. Three days earlier all four had entered the United States illegally. The aliens had then gone to Los Angeles on their second day in the country and had spent $150, buying fraudulent Social Security cards.

But the arresting officer had noticed that each of the cards was printed with the exact same Social Security number, yet all of the cards had a different name on them. So that particular apprehension was a good example of how the fraud, in the early 1990s, was exploding on us. After IRCA had been enacted in 1987, such occurrences began to incrementally increase each year. This meant that we were soon overwhelmed, and it became a bit unbelievable.

One only has to look at the statistics. In 1993 we made 4473 apprehensions in the Blaine sector, which was the most recorded of any other sector on the northern border. It's also important to point out that there were a number of cities across the U.S. where illegals could buy fraudulent documents besides Los Angeles. Chicago was another such location. Any place where there was active people-smuggling going on had such forgery centers. It was a big underground network, and the illegals knew where to go because the alien smugglers who'd brought them across the border would steer them to one of their contacts. That would be included in their smuggling deal.

Of course, law enforcement would regularly bust the forgers. That happened fairly frequently. But because the black market in fraudulent documents was so lucrative, another forgery mill would quickly pop back up in the busted one's place. There was a lot of it going on due to all of the money that could be made off the undocumented workers.

Now again, going back to what the law required in regards to filling out the I-9 Form, all a person had to do was simply present a document to an employer. For example, if a business was advertising for new hires and someone showed up to apply, the employer was only required to ask for a document. Then if the new hire had a Social Security card, the employer might suspect that it was fraudulent, but the employer was off the hook because of how the law had been written. In other words, there was no E-Verify requirement in IRCA that mandated any sort of vetting of the document's authenticity. An employer only had to *see* the document. They didn't have to actually check its legitimacy per any sort of confirmation via a phone call to a government agency or via a database follow-up.

If the employer was later asked why his business had hired an illegal alien, he might say, "I'm not an expert in documents. I couldn't tell it wasn't a good document." And this meant that even bad forgeries could be presented to an employer to get a job. It was a glaring loophole in the immigration law.

The second thing which happened was—some of the employers would count every employee as a subcontractor. That meant it was up to the subcontracting company to check to see if someone had a valid document to work in the U.S. So this was another way around the requirement. And, needless to say, it became really obvious in the 1990s that illegal immigration was completely out of control.

Also, when our officers would examine the documents—the forgeries were glaringly obvious. It didn't matter if it was a fraudulent birth certificate, Social Security card, or driver's license. Back then, for $125 to $150, someone could get a fake Social Security card and a forged California driver's license, both at the same time. It was easy to get a package deal. And that pretty much meant that any person who bought such forgeries could get a job.

Now, to their credit, there were a number of employers that actually did a good job of vetting who they would hire. This occurred because the E-Verify program had been made available as an option. But the program was voluntary, not mandatory. And many of the employers that used the E-Verify system did so because they didn't want to go through the expense of training a group of people to work for them and then have the Border Patrol come in and take those people away. If that happened, they'd have to spend more money and train yet another group of employees. So some of the employers realized that it was to their advantage to properly vet their new hires.

Nevertheless, during this particular time period, I was really getting frustrated since it seemed as though there was nothing being done to curtail the constant influx of illegal aliens. The only solution appeared to be to simply hire more Border Patrol agents. But I felt very strongly that the best way to stop the flood of undocumented workers into the U.S. was to shut off the job magnet. If the politicians truly wanted to prevent such people from coming to our country, then they needed to pass a law so that the *employers* that were hiring the illegal aliens had to face some legal consequences for knowingly ignoring the law. One report estimated that forty percent of the illegal aliens who were working in the U.S. had not come across the border illegally. Forty percent of them had actually come here as visitors and had just remained in the U.S. and hadn't gone back home when their visa had expired.

So, knowing what I knew in regards to the gaping holes in our immigration policies, I'd become more and more disheartened. I'd seen a lot of abuse in reforestation and in the other industries—where we'd go in and check and find fraudulent documents that were quite obvious to the eye. Again, all an employer had to say was that the person's document had looked good to them, and then the employer was off the hook.

Anyway, in June of 1993, I took a two-week vacation. I went home to Wyoming because my father was dying of cancer. My mother had told me that he didn't have much longer to live. Our kids were out of school, and so I took my wife and family on a trip to see my parents. Along the way, we also stopped to see my wife's parents for several days.

My dad was in a hospital in Afton, Wyoming. He lived about 25 miles from there. So on a Friday, after I'd been on vacation for about four days, I went to the hospital to spend time with my dad.

Then later, when I got back to my parents' house, my mother told me that my boss had called. His name was Tom Wacker. At that time, I was a GS-12; and my job title was the assistant chief.

So I stepped into the den, closed the door, and called Tom back. He told me, "Gene, earlier today I got a call from the acting chief of staff at the Immigration Service at our D.C. headquarters. On Wednesday of next week, the House Operations Committee will be holding a special hearing. It's going to cover illegal aliens working in the reforestation industry. The acting chief of staff has to go and testify at the Congressional hearing. You're recognized as the service's expert when it comes to reforestation."

I said, "Tom, Keith Miller is probably more up to speed on reforestation than I am, even though I've been heavily involved with it. Plus, I'm on annual leave. My dad's in the hospital, and he's not expected to live much longer."

Tom said, "Well, Mike Williams, the acting chief of staff, wants you there."

And that's when I realized how important the call really was. "Chief, I don't have a dress uniform with me. I don't have a suit."

"Gene, I've been ordered by the acting chief of staff to order you to be at our headquarters in D.C. on Monday morning."

When Tom told me that, I didn't have a choice in the matter. On Sunday we drove to the closest airport, which was in Salt Lake City. After I bought a new suit, my wife put me on a plane; and she took our kids and went to Northern Utah to visit her family.

On Monday morning I arrived at the Immigration Service's headquarters in D.C. and met with the chief of staff. He had me brief him and told me that he thought we'd have a lot of questions to answer at the hearing.

I spent Monday and Tuesday at the headquarters, and on Wednesday we went over to one of the Congressional hearing rooms. When I walked in the door, I noticed there were several tables set up. One table was for the Forest Service, and sitting at it was the Forest Service's representative whom I'd worked with in our region. He'd been involved in the coalition which I'd put together, and we had worked really well together in regards to the reforestation program.

A few feet away was another table where the coordinator for the Bureau of Land Management was sitting. And there was also a third table where the representative for the U.S. Department of Labor was sitting. He'd been part of the team which we'd brought in to handle the labor violations.

As I walked over to a fourth table that had been reserved for the INS, I noticed that it only had one microphone and that my assigned chair had been positioned behind the acting chief of staff's chair. So this seating arrangement was different than the way all of the other tables had been set up. It meant that the members of Congress, who were conducting the hearing, could not ask me a direct question, nor would I be sworn in. I also remember thinking, before I'd walked into the room, that maybe there was a silver lining. I was hoping I would be allowed to express some of my frustration and tell the congressmen how I thought they could solve the problem with illegal aliens and the reforestation industry, which was prevalent everywhere in the country. I had intended to tell them that what Congress needed to do was to set up some kind of national database so that employers would have to use a mandatory ID verification system.

Well, that didn't happen because I was never given the chance to offer my opinion. Instead, what did occur was that they would ask the acting chief of staff a question. For example, they'd say, "Mr. Williams, what is your estimated percentage of illegals who are working in the timber industry in the Pacific Northwest?"

Pausing before answering such a question, Williams would then turn around and whisper to me, "What do you think?"

I would say, "Seventy-five percent."

He'd then turn back around and say, "Seventy-five percent."

In other words, the INS had intentionally seated me off-mic since they wanted to control everything that was said. The higher-ups in my own agency did not want people who worked in the field, such as myself, to have an opportunity to tell Congress what really needed to be done. That was the way the whole hearing had been set up. My own agency had wanted to limit what I said. They didn't want me to be clear and explain how our work out in the field was actually being done.

So I was completely shut off and couldn't offer my frank opinion. Now, one would've thought, since this was playing out in front of members of Congress, that they would've been disturbed by how the process was being so tightly controlled. Yet, for whatever reason, none of them had attempted to correct what was transpiring right in front of them.

Consequently, I think it's interesting to point out that during my 30 years of government service—I never talked to another supervisor in the field who had ever testified before a Congressional hearing. Of course, there may've been some union representatives who'd gone before

Congress to offer their opinions on personnel issues; but as far as a field supervisor being brought in to testify about a policy issue—well, such a boots-on-the-ground practical sharing of real-world experience didn't happen as far as I was aware of.

On the Thursday after the hearing, I flew back to Utah and picked up my family. But sadly, I never saw my dad again. He died the first week in July. To this very day, that has always stuck in my craw. I deeply regretted not being there to spend more time with my dad. It really upset me because I knew the higher-ups could have sent any one of the other supervisors who'd worked in reforestation. But, of course, I'd been involved in negotiating the agreement with the National Forest Service, which meant I had a good bit of national name recognition. Still, I thought being with my dad when he was dying was more important, yet obviously the higher-ups didn't think the same way as I did in that regard.

I'd also like to again point out that when I entered on duty with the Border Patrol in 1971, there were only around 1500 Border Patrol agents for the entire United States. Then as the years passed and the numbers of un-documented aliens skyrocketed, the go-to solution which was implemented by the pencil pushers in D.C. was the hiring of more agents and the purchasing of more equipment. There never was any effort to cut off the job magnet.

I liken the situation to the U.S. Capitol Building catching fire due to a natural gas leak. Firemen and firetrucks are quickly rushed in to put out the blaze. But the flames continue to grow stronger and stronger. So more firetrucks are called and more firemen are dispatched. Yet no attempt is ever made to shut off the ruptured gas line, which means the fire is never brought under control.

The job magnet for undocumented aliens is analogous to that type of spewing gas line. We have gone from 1500 Border Patrol agents to 22,000 agents, and illegal immigration continues to be out of control. Mandatory E-Verify is what is needed to mitigate the magnetic pull of millions of jobs in the U.S.

Anyway, after returning from the Congressional hearing in 1993, I continued to feel that the Border Patrol was fighting a losing battle. And I thought the best way for Congress to turn the situation around was for the employment magnet to be taken away by some sort of national registry. I felt we needed a comprehensive database which could vet workers; and I also thought it should be mandatory since that would be the only way to control the hiring of illegal aliens.

Then the following year, the U.S. Commission on Immigration Reform—i.e., the Jordan Commission—submitted its report to Congress. The U.S.C.I.R. was headed by Congresswoman Barbara Jordan from Texas. The committee had four Democrats and four Republicans; and its report came out in September of 1994.

Now, in all honesty, I don't recall how I stumbled onto the Jordan Commission Report; but somehow I did. Then when I read through it, I noticed that the main cornerstone of its immigration reform was the recommendation that a mandatory verification system be used to vet Social Security numbers when an employer hired new employees. Plus, as I explained in the previous chapter, there were a number of other implementations which the report recommended because it also referenced a well-thought-out list of illegal-immigration issues.

The bottom line was—the report clearly stated that the *job magnet* needed to be taken away as a means to control illegal immigration. And I fully agreed. By cutting off the available jobs, Congress could quickly mitigate the illegal aliens that were flooding into the U.S. And the same would apply to overstays, too, i.e., to aliens who arrive on a temporary visa and then overstay the amount of time they've been granted here.

So if the legislation drafted by the Jordan Commission would have been enacted by Congress—I don't think we'd have as many undocumented aliens crossing our borders, and their numbers would eventually greatly diminish.

Also, an insightful observation which I'd like to emphasize, yet again, about the Jordan Commission was Barbara Jordan's summation. Here's a quote from the report that was submitted by the U.S. Commission on Immigration Reform to Congress: "The credibility of immigration policy can be measured by a simple yardstick: people who should get in, do get in; people who should not get in are kept out; and people who are judged deportable are required to leave." I think this statement clearly implied a need for E-Verify.

Hence, after I read the report, I thought its findings had hit the nail right on the head. And despite the fact that I never was one to write letters, that's exactly what I proceeded to do. I sat down and wrote the Immigration Commission a letter. In it I said, "I just want you to know, in my 25 years of experience, along with dozens of years in the field, that I want to congratulate you as a commission because you have absolutely identified the problem and a solution to the problem."

I sent that letter off. The executive director of the Jordan Commission, at that time, was Susan Martin.

Then several months later, which probably would have been in January or February of 1995, I received a reply back from Susan Martin. It was an official letter, and it thanked me for offering my opinion. I was told that Barbara Jordan had read my letter and that she'd really appreciated it.

Seven months after I'd received Susan Martin's letter—in September of 1995—I was still the assistant chief. One day I was in my office; and I got a phone call from the area port director for immigration, i.e., from the administrator who managed our ports of entry. It was Gerry Blotsky. He said, "Gene, the Jordan Commission is in Canada. They're meeting right across the border at White Rock, and they want you up there ASAP."

Now, when Gerry called me, I was temporarily serving as the acting chief since the regular chief was out of town. And I was stunned to learn that the entire Jordan Commission was that close to where I was. White Rock, British Columbia, was only 26 miles north of Bellingham.

So, as requested, I drove across the border. It should be noted that one of the commission members was a guy named Harold Ezell. Ezell was a wealthy businessman who'd started Der Wienerschnitzel, which was a fast-food chain in California. He'd been appointed during the Reagan administration when Alan Nelson was the Commissioner of the INS. Ezell was the Regional INS Director for the Western Region, which covered all of California. Plus, he was a huge fan of the Border Patrol. Harold Ezell loved the Border Patrol. He used to go out and do ride-alongs with Border Patrol agents.

So I arrived a little late in White Rock, and I was told that Ezell's first question at the meeting had been, "Where is the Border Patrol? I need to talk to a representative from the Border Patrol because they're the only ones that really know what's going on on the border. INS doesn't know that much about it. If I want to know what's actually happening between the United States and Canada, I need to speak to someone from the Border Patrol."

I then entered the room where the committee was meeting and introduced myself to Harold Ezell since I had never met him before. I told him I was from the Border Patrol.

He said, "Where have you been?"

I said, "Sorry I'm late, but I was just notified about this less than an hour ago."

"What? They just notified you?"

"Yes, sir."

Ezell rolled his eyes and then introduced me to Susan Martin.

Of course, I instantly knew who she was; and I told her, "Susan, you may not remember the letter I wrote you; but I wrote you one a number of months ago."

She said, "Yes, I remember that letter. Please, come over here. I'd like to introduce you to Barbara Jordan." Ms. Martin then stood up and led me across the room.

I followed Susan Martin to where Barbara Jordan was seated. I'd never met the Congresswoman before; but I had seen pictures of her, from years earlier, when she was on the Watergate Commission. And regrettably, Barbara Jordan was now sitting in a wheelchair.

Walking up to Barbara Jordan, Ms. Martin said, "Barbara, this is Assistant Chief Davis. You may remember the letter he sent us."

Barbara Jordan turned towards me, and I explained to her, "I want to personally thank you, Ms. Jordan. I want to commend you and the commission for the job you did. In my twenty-five years of experience, I think you hit the nail right on the head. If Congress wants immigration reform, you've covered all aspects of it; and I congratulate you on a job well done."

Barbara Jordan nodded her head and said, "Would you please come over here for a minute?"

When I walked over to her, she stood up out of her wheelchair, put her arms around me, and pulled me closer. She looked me in the eye and said, "You have no idea how much that means to me because I can't get anyone in Immigration to acknowledge our report in D.C."

And when she told me that, I said, "I don't mean to be frank, but since you're wheelchair bound, the effort it must take to travel all throughout the country and outside the country to do this type of work—I'm just amazed that you would take on such an important position."

She said, "Well, let me tell you something. When they first offered me this job and asked me if I would do it, I was inclined to turn it down. But then when I had more time to think about it, I knew I could not turn it down. And I felt that way because illegal immigration in the United States affects my own people—black African Americans—more than any other class of people. It takes jobs away from them. I could not live with myself if I refused to be part of this important work."

And ever since that day, her words have haunted me. She told me that in September of 1995; and four months later she was dead. She died of pneumonia in Austin, Texas.

Now, to fill in some of the other details on what happened that day in White Rock, I did address the commission; and I was quite impressed by the bipartisanship of its eight members. The Democrats and Republicans seemed to genuinely like each other. They would joke with their fellow colleagues.

So when I stood up to briefly explain my thinking, I offered them an off-the-cuff opinion since I hadn't had any time to prepare a formal statement. I said, "I've already told Ms. Jordan that I've read your report and I commend you on a job well done."

Barbara Jordan clapped her hands and said, "And I didn't even bribe him to say that."

Of course, I was very moved by the whole experience; and I will never forget the exchange I had that day with Barbara Jordan. As I've frequently stated, I thought every aspect of the commission's report was spot-on. Congress should have listened to their bipartisan advice. But the report was completely ignored, and this was partly due to the fact that some of the higher-ups at INS were not on the same page with the Border Patrol due to the fact that the INS commissioner had always been a political appointee. For many years, lobbyists had been trying to influence the agency's policies. There were also a number of published articles which claimed that the U.S. Chamber of Commerce was the biggest lobbying group that was working against immigration reform. And such a response would've been because the U.S. Chamber of Commerce represented thousands of businesses that had illegal aliens working for them, which meant that influential organization was well aware of what would happen if such a low-paid workforce wasn't available to its members.

So, in my opinion, I thought the public should be told what was actually going on behind the scenes; and that's why I wanted to write this book.

Anyway, back in 1995, I felt there might have been a little serendipity to what had occurred after I'd mailed off my letter to the Immigration Committee—which I'd done several months before the Jordan Commission had showed up in White Rock, British Columbia. In other words, to have the Immigration Commission suddenly end up right up the road from where I worked . . . seemed to me to be as though it was almost one of those things that was meant to be.

-12-

When the first terrorist case occurred in the Blaine sector, we had an intelligence unit which consisted of two people. And so I immediately wanted to know if what had happened would be a one-time event or if we actually had the potential to have a recurring problem with terrorists coming into the United States from Canada.

Consequently, working with the Vancouver Police Department and the Royal Canadian Mounted Police (the R.C.M.P.), our intelligence officers identified 55 terrorist organizations in Vancouver, Canada, which had some sort of presence there and which they thought we needed to be concerned about. That's also when we started doing reports, following up leads, and talking to various law enforcement officers in Canada. We took this approach because we knew it was much easier for foreign aliens to get into Canada than into the United States.

I would also like to point out that, around this time, our anti-smuggling unit processed a couple of very significant human-smuggling cases. These particular incidences involved illegal aliens from countries such as India. People were being brought into the United States from Canada with fraudulent documents; so this was, in fact, international human trafficking.

To further clarify—Canada is a very liberal country due to its welcoming immigration policies. The Canadian government actually wants to increase its country's population, fairly rapidly, since it has such a large landmass and since Canada has a relatively low-density of citizens in many places. Yet there has always been the associated problem of people simply using Canada as a convenient stepping stone in order to illegally enter the United States.

Thus, in this regard, the U.S. Border Patrol has had to be diligent in preventing the lone individual—who might not have anyone else helping him—from improperly crossing into the United States. Our officers also have had to police the human smugglers who are attempting to bring groups of people in from Canada.

Now, when the statistics are looked at, the Border Patrol's apprehensions did, indeed, fluctuate over the years. For example, in 1993 we made about 4400 apprehensions at the Blaine sector. In 1994 we had almost 4000 apprehensions. But then in 1996 it dropped to a little over 2000. And in 1997 the apprehension rate was about the same. This was because 50% of the manpower that we had at the Baine sector had been detailed down to work on the southern border. So because we were hampered by a personnel shortage, we knew we had a lot of people crossing in from Canada, which we weren't catching during that particular segment of years.

I would also like to state, per the political debate over building a new wall along our southern border, that such a humongous construction project would require a huge amount of money and, in my opinion, those many billions of dollars would be better spent if the tax money was used to enhance our surveillance systems instead. Yet there's no doubt that a more advanced wall is, in fact, needed in certain urban areas like San Diego and Nogales. That's true because it's so easy to cross into those sprawling overbuilt areas and then quickly get lost in the crowds.

But a wall that would run the whole length of the southern border is not realistic; and I think advocating for that type of a massive structure is flawed thinking. Investing so much taxpayer money into building such a steel/concrete behemoth that would loom over the 1,954 miles of our southern border isn't practical. There are many isolated areas where it'd be totally uncalled for. Of course, I probably would not have said this at the time I retired at the end of 1999. Back then, we probably only had about 6,000 Border Patrol agents on duty. But now we have something like 22,000 Border Patrol agents protecting our international borders 24/7. Plus, we have advanced technological systems, such as high-flying drones and a number of other electronic enhancements to help mitigate the influx of illegals from Mexico.

Also, another border-crossing aspect that has significantly changed between the time I worked on the southern border—in the 1970s—and now . . . is that back then there were basically two different groups of people who were coming across the border. There were the smugglers that smuggled aliens, and there were the smugglers that smuggled drugs. In other words, at that time the cartels did not have control of the U.S.-Mexico border. Yet now the cartels do, in fact, have control of many parts of our southern border. And the cartels are not only in control of the drugs coming into this country, they're also supervising the people smuggling as well. The cartels are using 18-wheelers to transport thousands of illegal aliens into the U.S. interior, i.e., to move large groups of people up from the Mexican border. I've seen news reports that undocumented aliens are paying as much as $6500 to be smuggled into the United States.

This means that human smuggling has gotten to be so lucrative that the drug cartels are using this revenue stream as another way to make large sums of money. Bringing illegal aliens into our country has become quite profitable for organized crime.

Now, in my opinion, if we really want to stop illegal aliens and drugs from being smuggled across the border, then I think our politicians should take one fourth of the tax money that it would take to build a new wall and use those funds to put in a computer system to implement E-Verify instead. If they did that, such an investment would put a stop to the employment magnet. But again, the U.S. Chamber of Commerce and the cheap-labor lobbyists do not want to weaken the present status quo. So the new super wall is a bit of a hoax. It's a way to con the public into thinking that the problem will be solved—when it won't actually be solved at all. Illegal aliens will still be able to find a way over the wall or under the wall, and the unrelenting deluge of undocumented workers into the U.S. will continue.

To be clear, I think our politicians are avoiding what truly needs to be done. A humongous wall will not solve the problem, whereas E-Verify would quickly put a stop to people coming here for low-paid jobs.

Years back, an ex-chief of police over on the Kitsap Peninsula in Washington State told me something that few people ever think about. He said when he'd put in for his Social Security benefits after he'd retired, it was only then that he had found out there were five other people who'd been using his Social Security number. This meant that he was restricted to receiving only a partial monthly payment until the Social Security Administration was able to properly sort out what his correct reimbursement amount actually should be due to the multiple-usage irregularities of his benefit's account.

I'm also reminded of another similar situation. A guy I used to work with at the Border Patrol had retired and had moved back to California. Then about four years ago, he'd filled out his taxes and had sent in the forms. A few weeks later he got a letter back from the IRS, which had denied a portion of his claim. The denial was based upon his wife's Social Security number. My friend was told that an earlier tax form had been mailed in and that a refund had already been processed and issued. As it turned out, a crook had stolen his wife's identity. This had happened because there was no communication between the IRS and the Social Security Administration. So every year, for the following three years, when my friend wanted to file his taxes—he had to go to the IRS to get a new number to use on the forms in order to make sure his wife's refund wouldn't be stolen.

Of course, there are literally millions of such fraud cases going on in this country each year. That's why if our politicians simply took a fourth of the money that would be needed to build a new border wall and used those funds to implement an E-Verify database instead, such an enhanced employment system would, I think, be a slam dunk. It's a no-brainer. And then once that new system is put in place, it would prevent a lot of identity fraud and quickly stop illegal aliens—who don't have any legitimate documentation to get a job—from flooding into the U.S.

It should also be pointed out that back when the new wall along our southern border was first proposed and it began generating a lot of press in 2016—there was some initial interest by President Trump and certain politicians to actually implement an E-Verify system. But then E-Verify was pulled off the table, and the politicians stopped advocating for it. This happened because the lobbyists for cheap labor began twisting arms on Capitol Hill. And now E-Verify is not even mentioned by the politicians who had previously been pressing for its implementation. Indeed, back in 2017, E-Verify was one of the so-called pillars of the administration's immigration reform. But soon that pillar suddenly disappeared from the White House's agenda.

Then later, as the pages of the calendar changed and the months progressed into 2018, the Center for Immigration Studies was the only organization that I knew of which was still actively promoting the E-Verify reforms. Whenever I would meet someone and I'd tell them I used to work for the Border Patrol, the first question they would always ask me tended to be: *What do you think about the proposed new wall?*

I would tell them that I thought a wall is, indeed, needed in a number of urban areas; but that it would be way too costly and wouldn't work in many of the other less-populated regions along our southern border. Plus, I'd also tell them that I didn't think a huge wall would actually be needed in any of the urban areas if there wasn't a job magnet pulling so many illegal aliens into our country.

To again be clear, I personally believe that we do, in fact, need physical barriers to stop illegal-alien vehicles at many spots on the border. That's true. Yet I also think we should concentrate on employing a lot more drones— along with adding extra electronic surveillance devices— especially in regards to the drug smugglers. But still, with the number of Border Patrol agents which we presently have, if E-Verify was implemented, then the job magnet would be cut off within a very short amount of time.

-13-

In June of 1996, a pair of park rangers apprehended two individuals at Ross Lake—which is in the North Cascades National Park in Washington State. The two hikers had walked across the Canadian border and were hypothermic. One guy was named Abu Mezer. He'd gotten separated from his friend, who was named Jamal Abed. When the park rangers had asked them where their car was, the hikers had given them different stories. The two had initially told the officers that they'd left their car on the Canadian side and had walked into the United States. But then later, they said they didn't have a car. So it was obvious to the park rangers that these two had been dropped off.

Abu Mezer said he was a Palestinian, and he also claimed he was a citizen of Jordan. Jamal Abed showed the National Park rangers a Washington State driver's license, which listed a Seattle address. He said he was a cabdriver. He had $500 in his wallet. That's when the officers surmised that Abed may have been smuggling Mezer into the U.S.

The park rangers then notified the Border Patrol. The following morning a Border Patrol agent from the Lynden station took custody of the two hikers.

When he was being questioned by the Border Patrol agent, Abu Mezer—besides claiming he was a Palestinian and a citizen of Jordan—also said he'd been admitted into Canada as a student. Jamal Abed claimed he'd been granted permanent residency in Canada and in the United States.

To verify their stories, the Border Patrol ran criminal record checks on each of them. No criminal records in Canada were found. A problem then arose because, at that time, trying to find jail space for such apprehensions was almost impossible. Detention funds were very low.

Now, normally, if the Border Patrol apprehended someone who'd entered the country illegally from Canada, the person would then be kicked back across the border if the Canadians would agree to take him or her back.

So a call was made, and that's what happened. The Canadians okayed it. Abu Mezer and Jamal Abed were both sent back to Canada.

Then a week later, a U.S. Border Patrol agent was sitting in his vehicle up by the Peace Arch Park in Blaine. Peace Arch Park is a fairly large park. Part of it is in the United States, and part of it is in Canada. The agent noticed a guy with headphones covering his ears. He was carrying a Walkman with him as he jogged through the cross-border greenspace of the park. The guy then entered the United States from Canada illegally since he hadn't checked in at a port of entry.

Having noticed what had happened, the Border Patrol agent hurried over and stopped the jogger. It was Abu Mezer, and he was taken into custody. When the agent ran his name through the computer system, he saw the previous record of an Abu Mezer having been caught at Ross Lake a week earlier. Yet this time Mezer had a completely different story. And that piqued the agent's interest, and he suspected that Mezer might be scouting out a smuggling route. But as had happened the first time he was apprehended, there wasn't any jail space available to hold Abu Mezer due to the U.S. budget cutbacks.

So again, our officer called the Canadians. A background check was run, and no criminal record was found on Abu Mezer. He was kicked back to Canada a second time. The Border Patrol also wrote up a report on him due to his suspicious activities, but there was nothing that could be proven in regards to us keeping him locked up.

Then about six months later, Darryl Essing—who was a Border Patrol agent at our Bellingham station—was doing a transportation check by himself one night. It was about 10:30 p.m., and Darryl had gone to the Bellingham Greyhound bus station. There, he saw three individuals who were staring out the glass door and who seemed sort of out of place. When the three noticed Darryl's patrol car outside, they backed away from the door and walked over to the other side of the lobby.

Darryl had a gut suspicion that he needed to talk to the three guys. But since he was working by himself, he waited until the next Greyhound bus had arrived. And that was when he pulled his patrol car up and parked it a few feet in front of the bus. He did this as the three guys were walking over to the door of the bus, which meant that Darryl had hemmed the guys in between the two vehicles.

Quickly hopping out of his patrol car, Darryl confronted the three guys. Then suddenly, one of the guys tried to get away; and Darryl ran over and grabbed ahold of him. It didn't take Darryl long to handcuff all three of them and take them into custody.

Now, as it turned out, the one who had tried to split was Abu Mezer. After Darryl had taken the three of them back to the office, he got on the phone and talked to the Canadians. He found out that Abu Mezer actually did have a record for simple assault and theft.

To this day, I don't know why Mezer's previous arrests up in Canada hadn't been uncovered when the Canadians had been called the first two times. I don't know if the Canadians hadn't run the earlier record-check inquiry properly or what had actually happened.

Anyway, it was a screwup; and now the Canadians said they would not take back any of the three guys. One of them claimed he was a Jordanian, like Mezer; and the other one said he was an Iranian.

Then after Darryl had processed them, he set up deportation hearings for the threesome, which meant that they would not be released from custody. He also intended to send them to Seattle for detention and thus let the office down there sort out what needed to be done next.

Darryl called me around midnight. I had the authority to set bond anytime anyone was being placed in jail. He told me he had the three guys in custody. He also said that one of the guys, Abu Mezer, had been apprehended by us before and that there was something suspicious about the guy. Darryl said, "I don't have a good feeling about him. I'm going to call the FBI because I think the FBI should talk to him. It's just a gut feeling I have."

I said, "Go ahead and do it." I then set a $15,000 bond on Abu Mezer, which normally would have been a $5000 bond. And, if I remember correctly, I think I put $10,000 on the other two. I would also like to point out that I was actually limited on the amount of bond that I could set, and $15,000 was pretty much the maximum I could assess in such a case. The average would've been $5000 since most of the illegal aliens we processed didn't have a way to come up with that amount of money anyway.

Darryl then called the Bellingham FBI and left a message on their phone. He told them that he was booking Abu Mezer into jail and he also gave the FBI the background information he'd uncovered.

A couple hours later, after Darryl had finished writing up his paperwork, he went over to the FBI's office and slid his apprehension report under their door so they would have it.

When one of the FBI agents came in the next morning, he listened to Darryl's phone message and erased it. That particular FBI agent had decided not to respond to the Border Patrol's request. And, to this day, I don't know why that FBI agent had handled it the way he had.

So the three guys, including Abu Mezer, were sent to Seattle. And once Mezer arrived down there, he claimed that if the U.S. deported him to Jordan, then the Jordanians would say that he was a member of Hamas because the Israelis had a record of him being involved in the Intifada. Mezer had lost a finger, which had been shot off. He was worried he'd be prosecuted for being a member of Hamas—which he swore wasn't true—even though our officers later found out that he actually did have ties to Hamas terrorists.

Now, when Abu Mezer went to his immigration hearing, his attorney told the judge that Mezer wanted to apply for political asylum. That was when the immigration judge lowered the bond on him to $5000. Abu Mezer was then kept in custody for about a month, before some guy from Seattle showed up with $7000 in cash. This meant Mezer's money guy had the $5000 to post for the bond and another $2000 leftover for incidentals. When asked, the guy had said that the money had come from Mezer's uncle who lived in Saudi Arabia.

It was later discovered that the person who'd posted the bond was subject to arrest for violating his immigration status. Mezer's money guy had been admitted into the United States as a college student but had never actually attended school. For some reason, his status hadn't been checked when he'd showed up at the Seattle INS office.

So Abu Mezer bonded out, and he continued to say that he wanted to apply for asylum. I think he stayed in Seattle for a couple of months while they attempted to set some hearing dates on him. Finally, through his attorney, he notified the immigration court that he was going to voluntarily leave the country since he'd changed his mind about pursuing asylum.

And that was when Abu Mezer suddenly disappeared, and we didn't hear anymore from him.

But approximately six months later, when I was driving to work one morning, my cell phone went off. It was an agent in Blaine. He said, "Gene, did you notice the national news this morning?"

I said, "Yeah."

The agent said, "So I guess you saw the lead story. The NYPD kicked in a door in Brooklyn this morning and shot two guys who were getting ready to do a double suicide attack with some bombs on the New York subway."

I said, "Yes, I saw that."

The agent then replied, "Well, the ringleader was Abu Mezer—the guy Darryl Essing arrested six months ago."

And that was when all hell broke loose. Rudy Giuliani, who was the mayor of New York City at the time, went to Janet Reno, the Attorney General; and she ordered an investigation. After the investigation had wrapped up, the Bellingham FBI agent—who hadn't responded to Darryl's phone message—was transferred to somewhere else.

Also, since Abu Mezer and the other Brooklyn bomber were only wounded and not killed when they were caught, those two ended up going to trial. And during the trial, Mezer suddenly stood up in the courtroom and started shouting all of this anti-Israeli propaganda. So that's when the media labeled him a lone-wolf terrorist.

But I disagreed with that assessment per my own analysis of his actions. I didn't think he fit the lone-wolf profile. In other words, when such a determined criminal like him had backup in place because someone with $7000 had stepped in to bond him out—and then he later ended up making a bomb in Brooklyn—well, to me that meant he had a network of people supporting him. So I knew he wasn't a lone wolf.

Here's an interesting side note. In 2012 I was in Kosovo. I was working for the State Department, and this was after I'd retired from the Border Patrol at the end of 1999. I had a presentation I did on terrorism, where I talked about different terrorism cases. One day I was talking about the Abu Mezer case, and I mentioned how it had been so screwed up per there having been a number of *red flags* that had been missed by our guys, which had allowed Mezer to be bonded out and later to be able to almost pull off a bombing in New York City.

Then shortly after I had finished explaining my take on what had happened with the Brooklyn bombers, a stranger came up to me. He introduced himself and said, "I listened to your presentation. I'm a retired deputy commander of the NYPD. I need to tell you the rest of the story."

I looked him straight in the eye and said, "What's the rest of the story?"

He said, "Well, what you said was exactly true. But there's a few things you don't know. And the only reason this other stuff eventually came out was because there was a third guy in that Brooklyn apartment with Abu Mezer. He was an Egyptian who'd been a green-card-lottery recipient, and he was trying to save money and bring his family over from Egypt. The thing was, he saw the bombs actually being made; but he didn't speak any English. So he'd fled the apartment and had desperately tried to find someone who spoke Arabic. He was able to get the attention of the cops, and they had an Arabic speaker talk to him. That was how the NYPD found out where the bombers were. And that's when the cops notified the FBI because the FBI had jurisdiction over all terrorism cases.

"Now, I know this might be hard to believe, but the FBI wasn't interested enough in the insider intel to provide assistance on the entry into the apartment. The NYPD did the entry themselves, and that's when they ended up shooting the bombers because they went for their guns. But there's also something else you'll be surprised to learn. In that apartment there were pictures of the Twin Towers; there were pictures of the Brooklyn Bridge; there were pictures of the subway train . . . and there were also documents showing that the rent was being paid by a terrorist organization. Then after the police had raided the place—the FBI arrived a little later, sacked up every bit of that stuff, put it in a brown box, and it never saw the daylight again."

Needless to say, I was a bit shocked by what that retired deputy commander of the NYPD had told me that day in Kosovo.

So, to be clear, the Abu Mezer incident was the first terrorism case the Border Patrol was involved with in our sector. And it's also important to note that our agents didn't have any prewarning or preparatory training in regards to such activities by terrorists.

Later, when I go into the details of our second terrorism case and explain our government's bureaucratic response to these types of events—the reader will, quite regrettably, begin to understand that there was a somewhat limited *reactive* mindset that only proceeded to get worse, not better, as time progressed per various federal agencies becoming more and more involved in such cases.

Now, after the Brooklyn bombers had been apprehended, we continued to detail Border Patrol agents from the northern border down to the southern border. Then one day, a couple of our agents came into my office and said, "Gene, we'd like to talk to you for a minute. We are so shorthanded that it's affecting our ability to do our jobs. There's stuff going on along the border; and we know it's happening; but we just don't have the manpower to do anything about it. We've been taking to our counterparts in the Royal Canadian Mounted Police, along with some agents in U.S. Customs; and we'd like to put a joint-taskforce team together."

I said, "That's a great idea. Let's do it."

And so, as tends to happen, a lot of these types of pragmatic ideas actually percolate up from the boots-on-the-ground guys. Indeed, this was how the Integrated Border Enforcement Team—a.k.a., I.B.E.T.—was first formulated. That's when we began strengthening our relationships with our Canadian counterparts. We started meeting with them on a regular basis. The Mounties would coordinate their patrols with us and go out on the exact same nights as our agents would on their patrols. We even used a big truck with a Starlight Scope for such assignments.

As a consequence, vis-à-vis this type of cross-border coordination, the Mounties would be on one side of the international border; and we would be on the other side. And somewhat surprisingly, we were astounded by the smuggling activity that was uncovered. We caught one guy with 26 guns that he was trying to sneak into Canada. We also stopped a load of cocaine from crossing north. So I.B.E.T. turned out to be very effective due to the fact that our officers went proactive, not reactive. In other words, we weren't simply waiting for something to happen, like in the Abu Mezer case. Instead, we were attempting to get ahead of the curve in order to stop the bad guys before they exited or entered the United States.

Hence, the foundation we laid—once we began working with the R.C.M.P. and U.S. Customs—really came into play when a second terrorism case was discovered in our sector, which involved a guy coming into the United States on the Port Angeles ferry from Victoria, British Columbia.

But even then, we were woefully ill-prepared. When our agents initially stopped that particular guy, they first thought he was smuggling drugs into the country, i.e., they simply assumed he was transporting illegal chemicals. They had no idea that it was actually explosives.

To better fill in the blanks, let me regress a little in order to further clarify a few of the accompanying circumstances surrounding our first terrorism case with Abu Mezer. Now, because his bombmaking threat had unfolded over a series of months, I was seriously troubled at how some of our law enforcement agencies had dropped the ball. I felt more could've been done to prevent an illegal alien with terrorist ties from entering the U.S. and thus being able to build a bomb. Yet in one respect, I can't say that the Border Patrol was at fault since we had, in fact, arrested Abu Mezer three different times. We had done our job. But still, the ball had been dropped because our agency didn't have the resources, nor did we have the jail space, nor did we have the budgetary funding to incarcerate such a border intruder as Abu Mezer—due to the fact that a lot of the illegal aliens, at that time, were being kicked back to Canada after we'd apprehended them. So our mode of response was reactive, not proactive—i.e., we were simply responding to a threat after it had occurred, instead of being able to prevent a terrorist episode from happening in the first place.

Still, a positive result was derived from the Abu Mezer case. It wasn't a lose-lose situation since the I.B.E.T. team had been formed in its aftermath. Our coordination with the Canadians had been ramped up at an opportune time due to the fact that the taskforce's inception was first initiated when there had been a precipitating unilateral operation, which the Border Patrol had begun on the Mexican border and which was called Operation Gatekeeper. This was when the higher-ups had started detailing our agents off of the northern border—even though we were shorthanded in the Blaine sector—and had begun moving them down to the southern border. And that redeployment of personnel had occurred because things had gotten completely out of control on our southern border. All of the emphasis was squarely focused, in 1996, on the enforcement area between Mexico and the United States.

So as we were *reacting* to the Abu Mezer incident, that was when I.B.E.T. was formed. And besides being initiated as an interagency group with U.S. Customs—we also worked with the R.C.M.P., Canada Immigration, and some of the local P.D.s. There was a strong emphasis on promoting cooperation between the various law enforcement agencies.

Now, what tended to typically happen—since we were so shorthanded on the northern border—was that the I.B.E.T. team would come to our Border Patrol sector headquarters, and they would check to see where we had a lot of sensor traffic occurring along the international boundary line. We maintained a 72-hour log of such activity.

Then when they found a heavily trafficked area, the team would go out and set up on both sides of the border. The Canadians would be in plainclothes units on their side; we would be staged on our side. And we were just astounded by the results. It was really an effective way of coping with the lawbreakers who were crossing back and forth between our two countries.

Another aspect that made this deployment technique so effective was the fact that it had been generated by the field agents themselves. They were the ones who'd come up with the idea for the coordinated effort. And luckily, as their superiors, we'd had the good judgment to implement what they had suggested to us. So it didn't take us long to realize how exceptionally productive such a coordinated team effort would be.

During I.B.E.T.'s first year, the team seized $1,000,000 in contraband—which included drug seizures, money seizures, and various other illegal items. We also had a number of major alien-smuggling cases, where people from China, India, and Korea had traveled into Canada and thus had used our northern neighbor as a jumping-off place to try to sneak into the United States.

Plus, another facet of our border enforcement, which was highlighted by the events of the Abu Mezer case, was the fact that Canada Immigration was so liberal with its immigration policies. The Canadians, in my opinion, were overly welcoming and very lax in regards to whom they let enter their country. And this was a big concern for us.

Again, in 1995, I think we had over 4000 apprehensions in the Blaine sector. Then in the following years, that number dropped by almost 2000, simply because we didn't have the manpower to properly protect the border. Yet a lot of the people in that lower apprehension figure were not processed by us as illegals who'd been caught coming across the border. Many of those undocumented aliens were apprehended vis-à-vis interior enforcement, which involved working the farm fields and reforestation.

So we were amazed at what we were getting on the northern border. Guns, cocaine, and U.S. currency were being smuggled up into Canada; and B.C. Bud and illegal aliens were being brought down into the United States. When we put the I.B.E.T. team together, I thought we'd made a number of smart decisions, even though we knew that having the two countries working closely together would concern some people, especially in regards to the sovereignty of both our countries. Indeed, certain people tend to get really upset when there are law enforcement officers from one country who are working inside the border of another country.

In addition to I.B.E.T., we also had I.B.I.T.—which was the Integrated Border Intelligence Team. That was a group of analysts who'd been brought in from each of the I.B.E.T. agencies, and these team members would analyze the data and intel which was gathered on both sides of the border. I.B.I.T. would then make strategic recommendations as to how the I.B.E.T. manpower should be used along the northern border. I'd also like to point out that I was very impressed by the Canadian Mounties. They did an excellent job. It truly was an honor to work with them.

Moreover, I think all of the I.B.E.T. members interacted exceptionally well together due to the strong professionalism of the personnel involved. The cohesion of the whole team was clearly obvious during I.B.E.T.'s first year of operation. The officers from the R.C.M.P.'s Vancouver region received an outstanding-job award from Ottawa. So I thought such a glowing recognition for work *well done* pretty much reflected upon all of the team members. Then after the 9/11 attacks, I.B.E.T. extended its reach to completely cover the northern border.

In regards to my personal involvement, I was the public information officer (i.e., the P.I.O.) for our sector at that time, along with being the assistant chief. This meant that I handled the press releases. Any time we'd have a significant event on the international border, I'd send out an info sheet, which involved anticipating the media's interest in our activities. So when I.B.E.T. was first formed, I contacted several news organizations and gave them a heads-up in regards to the coordinated effort between the U.S. and Canada. An explanation was offered that explained our limited resources on the border and how the newly formed cross-border team would enhance our effectiveness.

A good example of this was the placement of motion sensors. If an array of sensors was put on our side of the border in a targeted location, then the Canadians didn't have to invest their surveillance money for double coverage. Our sensors would alert us in regards to the foot traffic going both ways, and we would share that data with our Canadian counterparts.

Consequently, the efficient use of our limited patrol budgets was an important aspect when it came to both countries working together. The exchange of intelligence helped each country save money. And that was emphasized to the media.

Thinking back, I remember a correspondent for a local TV station in Vancouver, British Columbia—who'd actually gone out and ridden with the R.C.M.P. She was there one night when they seized 20 guns that were being smuggled across the border, and that news coverage was transmitted on the Canadian Broadcasting Corporation.

Now, even though we were having these types of success stories, I was still anticipating that at some point in the future there might be an issue with U.S. sovereignty. This meant we were constantly attempting to garner as much good publicity as possible, and that was part of my job as the public information officer.

There was also another border incident that demonstrated the effectiveness of the I.B.E.T. enforcement team. One night we had a group of 15 Korean women who were being brought in from Canada as prostitutes. In this trafficking situation, the smugglers were attempting to quickly walk the women into the United States. On the Canadian side, the Koreans had been driven to an out-of-the-way spot and dropped off. A load van was then waiting for them on the U.S. side of the border to pick them up. So this was organized human smuggling, but I never found out if it was an Asian or a Korean gang. Yet I did confirm that the attempt had initially been set up in Korea before the women had ever arrived in Canada.

Therein, this type of criminal activity was partly due to Canada's very liberal Visa Waiver Program, which meant that most foreigners didn't actually need visas to travel to Canada. They could simply fly into the country without having been issued a visa before departing their home country.

Anyway, as the public information officer, I had developed a number of media contacts. And during the whole time I had the job, I never lied to the press. I was always completely up front with them. If I couldn't explain something, I told them why I wasn't able to offer any more details on a specific topic. I never tried to deceive the press. I was honest, and I had a pretty good relationship with the media.

With the Korean-prostitute case, I did an interview with KIRO-TV out of Seattle. And by doing so—per employing a proactive approach—it allowed the Border Patrol's response to what had happened to be used in the news coverage.

Another time, the I.B.E.T. team had a case where a double kayak was loaded with B.C. Bud. The little boat had been paddled across Boundary Bay from White Rock, British Columbia; and we did a press release on that marijuana-smuggling arrest.

So by handling the border apprehensions in the way we did, it really paid off. Yet I also remember one particular instance that sort of fell through the I.B.E.T. cracks. This happened because there were certain nights, per the team's limited resources, when the Canadians didn't have anyone available on their side of the boundary line. One of those nights was a rainy, misty evening. We had an agent sitting in an unmarked vehicle on the U.S. side of the international border. We also had a K-9 unit parked nearby.

Striding out of the mist, a couple of backpackers approached the unmarked car. They were marijuana smugglers who were trying to backpack in some B.C. Bud. They'd mistaken our car for a smuggling car and had walked straight up to it.

Then when one of the backpackers suddenly realized his mistake, he quickly dropped his pack and took off running back into Canada. The dog was released from the K-9 unit and charged after him. But the problem was, we didn't have anyone deployed on the Canadian side. This meant that the K-9 officer had to go into Canada to retrieve his dog.

Well, when the officer got over into Canada, he saw that the dog had chased the smuggler up a tree. The smuggler was then taken out of the tree and arrested. Now, as one would expect, sovereignty instantly became an important issue. And that's when the K-9 officer contacted the local I.B.E.T. team, and they called the R.C.M.P. in Ottawa.

After being told what had happened, the Mounties said, "Screw it. Prosecute him."

And that's what we did. The backpacker had obviously broken laws on both sides of the border. Yet it was an interesting situation because, at that time, the biggest smuggler of B.C. Bud into the U.S. was the Canadian Hells

Angels. And even though the backpacker hadn't been wearing a leather jacket with the biker group's logo on it, the guy still could've been working for that violent motorcycle gang.

It's also important to note that the Canadian Hells Angels were one of the biggest producers of poultry chickens. This sideline business of theirs was important to them because if a surveillance plane was flying over a farming area and was looking for the heat generated by a marijuana grow house, the agricultural sheds where the chickens were being raised gave off the same amount of radiant heat as a grow operation; and that excessive heat could be picked up by a thermal-imaging detector. That's why the Hells Angels tried to conceal their marijuana grows by placing them beside one of their poultry farms.

So the above smuggling cases were examples of the northern border having its own unique policing parameters, which were quite different than those on our southern border. And in order to properly patrol the wilderness areas between the United States and Canada, it was advantageous for the Border Patrol to have a good relationship with the Canadian authorities. Plus, we knew we could trust the Mounties. It really lifted our spirits when various law enforcement officers from both sides of the border and from a variety of agencies interfaced with us, such as Customs and the DEA. We were all able to work quite well with each other under the Integrated Border Enforcement Team umbrella. Most of us had been assigned to the northern border for many years; yet none of us had ever worked with our counterparts from the other side of the border before. We knew each other, but that wasn't the same sort of interpersonal dynamic as would occur when we actually coordinated our efforts to solve a case. With the I.B.E.T. team, we'd really become brothers in arms.

So thank goodness our guys out in the field had come up with the idea to interact with the different agencies on both sides of the border. The added enthusiasm that I.B.E.T. generated among our officers was undeniable. We put some of the best people on our team for tearing apart cars and looking for concealed contraband. These were the customs inspectors who were stationed at the ports of entry. And the guys absolutely loved it. I.B.E.T.—all of a sudden—became the *in thing*. Everybody wanted to be a part of it.

But eventually our sector transitioned into yet another personnel phase. The chief I was working under, when we first put the Integrated Border Enforcement Team together, was Tom Wacker. Then we had a period of time when Tom was promoted, and he went back to the southern border as a higher-grade chief. We next had a guy who came in as the acting chief. But regrettably, the two of us did not get along very well together. He was one of those guys who immediately wanted to change things for change's sake. He was the type of person who wanted to move the furniture around just to show that a change had been made.

I remember when I'd done an info piece with one of the TV stations in Seattle, and I'd talked about the I.B.E.T. team and the Korean-smuggling operation which we'd busted up. At the time, I understood why we had Operation Gatekeeper and why there was a need to move a certain number of our officers down to the southern border on temporary details.

But previously under Tom Wacker, when he was our station chief, he'd tried to limit the number of agents which we would send south. Then the new acting chief came in with a different attitude. I think he had, more or less, told the higher-ups, "Ya'll just tell me how many agents you want, and they're yours." His response was irrespective of the needs of our own sector.

Whereas I took exception to that management style and told the new acting chief that we needed to keep more of our guys on the northern border. I also went to the media and explained why the Border Patrol should maintain its manpower levels in our sector.

Having ruffled some feathers, I got punished for sharing my opinion with the reporters. And since I was the assistant chief and since the new guy was the acting chief, he had the power to make those types of personnel decisions. Hence, I came in one day; and he told me, "Eugene, we are detailing you down to the southern border in thirty days."

I said, "Am I going down there as an assistant chief?"

He said, "No, you're not. We're sending you down as a patrol agent." Of course, that would've been a backhanded demotion, and it would've been a real struggle for me to deal with it.

Then, luckily for me, I got a phone call from one of my classmates who was the deputy chief at the San Diego sector. He said, "Gene, we usually don't do this. But if they send you south, we'll bring you in as an assistant chief down here."

As it turned out, instead of doing that, the acting chief who'd replaced Tom Wacker had ended up sending me to the regional office. And so every day, another officer and I had to go in, sit at a desk, and prepare all of the apprehension reports, which were given to the regional commissioner. That was my punishment for doing what I'd done, and it lasted for 30 days.

Then when I returned to the Blaine sector, the same acting chief—who'd wanted to send me south—had already brought in another person to serve as his acting deputy. This meant that all of my responsibilities had been shifted to that new deputy. So in one respect, I was on thin ice for a short period of time; and this was due to the fact that the acting chief had expected to be named the new chief relatively quickly.

But that's not what had happened. Instead of selecting him to be the new chief, the higher-ups had picked a guy named Carey James. Carey and I had worked together when I'd been detailed to Washington, D.C.; and Carey and I were good friends.

So Carey's first order of business when he got to Bellingham was to restore all of my duties and responsibilities. The acting chief who I hadn't gotten along well with—he had ended up transferring out of the Border Patrol and over to another position within the Immigration Service.

To further clarify, another reason I had been so outspoken in regards to our patrol agents being shifted around for Operation Gatekeeper . . . was because a couple of their wives had called me. I'd been told that it was really disruptive to their families for their husbands to be gone for thirty days—and then a month or so later—for their husbands to, yet again, be sent off on another temporary detail so far away from their homes. Conversely, I understood why the southern border needed the extra manpower because it was being overrun by a spike in the amount of illegal traffic that was crossing in from Mexico.

But I also was thinking about what had occurred with Abu Mezer on our northern border. It was still fresh in my mind. I was concerned about another such event and was frustrated that we might not be doing enough to prevent homicidal terrorists from entering the U.S. from Canada. And so, in one respect, if someone stepped back and looked at the big picture, there obviously was a funding issue that was hamstringing our personnel. We didn't have the needed resources to properly man both the northern and southern borders. Congress had not been allocating enough money to hire the required number of agents to do the job that needed to be done in order to safely control our international perimeters.

Therein, the service's plan to deal with the situation was to add more officers to the southern border. But at the same time, I was saying that we needed more patrol agents on the northern border, too. I thought the higher-ups were not looking at the big picture. After having dealt with our first terrorism case, I was concerned that we were detailing too many of our Border Patrol agents to the southern border. And even though I understood the logic behind temporarily shifting some of our supplemental manpower to handle the increased peak traffic that was coming up from Mexico, I still thought that our sector along the Canadian border was being shunned. Partly, this was due to the fact that I was getting reports from I.B.I.T., i.e., the intelligence team, that warned about more terrorism activity along our northern border.

Indeed, it eventually reached a point at the regional office—where we were sending our reports to—that the guys down there had started mocking us. They would say, "Oh, yeah, right. You've got a bloodthirsty *terrorist* hiding behind every tree." Then after a while, they finally told us, "We don't want any more reports with the *T* word. No more *T-word* reports. No more *T-reports,* understand?"

Of course, the proof was in the pudding. The southern border did, in fact, have dangerous cartel members who were crossing into the United States. Yet due to Canada's lax immigration laws, the worry was that another terrorist bomber, like Abu Mezer, would attempt to come in via the northern border.

Anyway, Carey James selected me to be his deputy chief, and we got along very well. Then a year and a half later, in July of 1998, I got a call from the public information officer for the Western Regional Immigration office. He told me that Martin Kasindorf had called him. Martin Kasindorf was a well-known reporter for *USA Today*, and he was doing research on Abu Mezer. Kasindorf also wanted to do an article about the northern border. The public information officer then proceeded to tell me that Kasindorf was coming up to Blaine and that the regional office wanted to send someone up to monitor his interview with me.

Needless to say, it really got my attention when I heard the information officer use the words: *"Monitor his interview with me."* I didn't think I needed anyone to monitor Kasindorf's interview, but I knew what the regional office was trying to do.

So when Martin Kasindorf showed up, he wanted to do a ride-along. I drove the patrol car, and Mr. Kasindorf rode up front with me. The assistant chief from the regional office sat in the back seat. Then after a few minutes of chitchat, Kasindorf asked to see the border area where Abu Mezer had crossed into the country at the Peace Arch Park in Blaine. Now again, this was in 1998, three years before 9/11; and I think Kasindorf, per his research and per having talked to a number of people, realized what the potential was for more such terrorist activities along the northern border. He knew we had less than 300 Border Patrol agents manning the whole length of the Canadian border—all the way to Maine. Martin Kasindorf was a very good reporter.

So as I drove him around and pointed out where Mezer had crossed in from Canada, the assistant chief from the regional office would say things like, "Mr. Kasindorf, are you aware of the border rescue units which we now have down on the southern border?" We'd then drive to another spot, and the guy in the back seat would say, "Mr. Kasindorf, are you aware of . . . (*this and that*)?" The assistant chief did this three or four times. He was constantly referring to the increase in trafficking activity along the southern border.

After Martin Kasindorf had spent most the day riding with us, he flew back to Los Angeles. The following day, I got a call from him. He said, "What in the hell was that guy in the back seat doing?"

I said, "He was trying to divert your attention away from the northern border and get it back on the southern border because the higher-ups are asking for more resources on the southern border and they're trying to control the story."

Kasindorf said, "The hell with them. I've already done a number of stories on the southern border. This one's on the northern border."

Then not long after that—when I got a call from a photographer—I should've suspected something important was about to happen. It was a news photographer, and he wanted to take some pictures of a few members of the I.B.E.T. team. So that's when P.J. Thompson and three other I.B.E.T. members, along with myself, met over at the stone border markers in Peace Arch Park and had the photos taken which Martin Kasindorf had requested.

About a week later on the front page of the *USA Today*, there was an article that had the headline: "Northern exposure." I think the reference to our *exposed* vulnerability was quite telling. The article dealt with the lack of resources on our northern border. It was excellent. Martin Kasindorf had done a great job.

This happened in July of 1998; and then on the 23rd of October—I had one of the lowest days in my career with the Border Patrol. That was the day that Scott Panchison, our pilot, crashed into Sumas Mountain. It was on a Friday; and Carey James, our chief, had originally planned an out-of-town trip. I'd talked to Scott on Thursday (the day before the crash) and had told him, "Carey's going out of town tomorrow. Let's fly over to Port Angeles. I need to do a station inspection."

So I was planning on flying with Scott the next day. But then at the last minute, Carey suddenly had changed his travel plans; and he'd scheduled a staff meeting. That meant I wasn't able to fly with Scott.

I guess it was around 3 o'clock in the afternoon on Friday, and I was sitting in my office in Blaine. The dispatcher called me. He said, "I don't want to alarm you, but a citizen has reported an airplane crash over on the west side of Sumas Mountain. I've been trying to get ahold of Scott. I haven't heard back from him. I can't get him on the radio, but I don't think it was him."

I told the dispatcher to call the Bellingham station and have them send one of their officers over to the airport. I said, "Tell them to check to see if Scott's car is still parked at the hanger."

So one of the guys drove over to the airport, and the dispatcher called me back. He said, "Scott's car is still there."

My heart sank. Carey and I then got into a vehicle, and we started driving toward Deming, which was near where the plane had gone down. Several minutes later, I got a cellphone call from one of our assistant chiefs. He said, "There was a timber company's helicopter flying in the area. They saw the smoke, and they landed their helicopter on a road. The copter pilot walked into the crash site. The only thing that was left of the plane was its tail, and it had our Border Patrol emblem on it." That eyewitness account meant that our Cessna 182 had, indeed, gone down.

To this day, I still get emotional thinking about it. When the assistant chief had explained to me that it was our plane, Carey and I both broke into tears and cried. Carey just wept.

Then once we'd gotten our composure back, we drove over to the crash site. The Whatcom County Sheriff's Department was already there. And what was so poignant was the fact that Scott had been in his early fifties and that he was such a great guy. He'd been a Marine carrier pilot in Vietnam. He had a master's degree. He was planning on retiring and then going back to teach school.

We were devastated.

Afterwards, we had a service for Scott. His memorial coincided with the national conference that the Border Patrol commissioner would schedule every year with the chief patrol agents. It was held in Texas. All of the chiefs and the INS commissioner flew in for the service, which was at a Christ the King Church. There were hundreds of officers from all over the country who attended it. I had the honor of conducting the service.

It was a really tough day when we lost Scott. It hit me pretty hard. We suspected that he probably had had a heart attack; but his body burned in the crash, which meant we never did know the exact cause of his death, although he had recently been complaining about pain and had been sweating a bit more than usual. The morning he'd crashed, I'd actually run into him in the office. He'd called me over to his desk to show me a new piece of equipment. We'd then had a brief conversation before he'd taken the plane up.

I remember how surreal it was—several hours later after Scott had passed away. Yet I knew there hadn't been anything wrong with the plane because it had recently been completely rebuilt. The Cessna 182 was just like a new airplane. I also talked to a woman who'd been an eyewitness. She'd watched the plane swoop by overhead, and she said it was flying level at a normal speed. She also said it had flown right into the mountain.

Of course, Scott's death was devastating for everybody. He was our link to the agents out in the field. As I mentioned before, all of our pilots in the Border Patrol had to first start their careers with us as regular patrol agents. Then they were later approved to be pilots.

So each day Scott would have coffee with the other agents. And if someone had a grievance, Scott would come and talk to me about it. He was my conduit to the guys who were patrolling the border. I really missed Scott.

Then about five months later, in March of 1999, was when I got a call from Congressman Lamar Smith's office in Washington, D.C. To fill in more of the details as to what proceeded to happen next, I should emphasize, yet again, that Lamar Smith was the chairman of the Judiciary Subcommittee on Immigration and Claims. Needless to say, I was quite aware of his reputation because he was such a giant when it came to immigration enforcement. I was familiar with his legislative efforts in Congress. He'd probably held dozens of hearings in regards to the problems with the Immigration Service and how it had broken down. Over the years, Congressman Lamar Smith had brought in numerous people to testify. His work had been very extensive on the subject.

Anyway, Lamar Smith's office called me and said that he would be holding a hearing on the need to put additional resources on the northern border. The congressman wanted to know if I would be willing to come in and testify at the hearing.

His office then talked to Carey James, who was still our sector chief at that time. Carey recommended that I fly to D.C. and testify. That was one of the things which I really liked about Carey James as the chief. A lot of the Border Patrol chiefs had big egos. So if there was going to be a major Congressional hearing, they would want to go and testify themselves.

But Carey wasn't at all like that. He told me, "Gene, you're the expert. You've worked on the northern border for many years. If anybody should go to D.C. and testify, it's you."

I took a moment to think about it and told him that I'd be willing to do it.

Carey then spoke to the Immigration Service, and they first told him I couldn't testify. He replied that Congressman Lamar Smith had specifically asked that I attend the hearing. So Carey wouldn't take *no* for an answer. He told the higher-ups that I would, in fact, go and testify.

I think that was when they finally realized how politicized the situation had become. They said, "Okay, Deputy Chief Davis can come to D.C., but he won't really testify."

Now, when Congressman Lamar Smith was told what the Immigration Service was planning on doing, he said, "No, I'll subpoena him; and he will, indeed, testify."

The higher-ups then said, "If Deputy Chief Davis is going to come to the hearing, we'll also have to bring in a chief from the Eastern Region." In other words, headquarters intended to bring in a chief patrol agent who had helped design a staffing plan, which specifically favored the southern border and which emphasized that region's needs to the detriment of the northern border. The agent they were bringing in had been a yes-man regional commissioner, and that was how they intended to balance out the testimony.

Lamar Smith said, "Okay, I'll agree to that."

Thereupon, as someone later told me, the higher-ups were obviously attempting to stop me. But thankfully they couldn't put the brakes on it because of the power that Congressman Lamar Smith wielded in Congress.

Still, I'd immediately become concerned when I was told what the higher-ups had said. I told Carey, "They're not going to be happy with my testimony." I thought this was true because I knew, before I could attend the hearing, that I would have to first go to the INS headquarters in D.C. and meet with the Congressional-liaison people. My main contact person was an attorney named Laura Baxter, and she worked for Lamar Smith. She had previously been with the Immigration Service, and so she was the one who was setting up the meeting.

Before leaving for D.C., I had told Laura Baxter on the phone, "I think they're going to try to crucify me. But still, I understand why they're trying to build up the southern border since it's completely out of control. Yet we've also got some serious problems up here on our northern border, too. So I'll be willing to testify on one condition."

"What's that?" she replied.

"The condition is—when Lamar Smith asks me his last question, I'd like him to mention my twenty-nine years of experience; and I'd like him to request my opinion as to what I think the solution is to solving the immigration problem. I want to talk about the Barbara Jordan Report. I want to talk about E-Verify. So if Congressman Smith will ask me that question, I'll agree to do it." I then went on to say, "But I'm sure they're going to try to bury me."

Laura Baxter said, "Listen, I can't tell you what's going on. But don't worry, we're going to take care of you. I promise you that."

"Well, I think you can understand why I'm so concerned because they're well aware of my reputation." Of course, I also knew I'd be retiring at the end of the year, and I knew that there wasn't much they could do about it.

The hearing was held in April of 1999. I flew to D.C. on the 12th, and on the 13th I went to the INS headquarters. I was familiar with the offices in that particular building because I had been detailed to INS years before, back during IRCA. Still, I felt somewhat out of place, even though

I actually knew the deputy chief of the Border Patrol and I got along with him pretty well.

The higher-ups assigned a guy to work with me, which involved him going over my statement. I then had to go to the commissioner's conference room. It was on one of the upper-levels. There, I met with some Congressional staff people who served as liaisons and who would brief people before they went to a hearing. I was then prebriefed about the committee's procedures.

The first thing they said to me was, "You'll be at the hearing, but we're not going to ask you a lot of questions because we know where you're coming from."

Needless to say, I understood right then and there that I was going to testify, which they did not actually want me to do. Whereas the main guy whom they were briefing was someone by the name of Michael Pearson. He'd just been appointed as the Associate Commissioner over all enforcement at INS. This was going to be the first Congressional hearing that he would testify at, which meant they were briefing him on the questions that might come up.

Also in the room was a chief of one the Border Patrol's eastern sectors. This was the yes-man whom they intended to use to explain why the staffing of the southern border should be the agency's top priority. In other words, there was no doubt what that Eastern Region guy was being brought in for.

So I would be sitting there in front of the Congressmen and Congresswomen as a participant witness. We were also told there'd be two separate groups. The A group would testify first, and the B group would testify second. The Congressional liaison, who was briefing us, then went on to explain that he was waiting to receive the final list as to whom would be in each group.

Then when we were about an hour into the briefing, the fax machine went off; and the Congressional liaison stood up and stepped over to it. Now, that morning before I'd gone in to be briefed, I'd touched base with Lamar Smith's office; and again they'd reassured me, saying that I shouldn't worry and that I'd be taken care of.

So getting back to when the fax machine had beeped and whirled—the Congressional liaison pulled the transmitted sheet of paper out of the machine and read it. When he did this, his whole countenance immediately changed. I mean, it was quite remarkable. It looked like all the wind had gone out of his sails. He turned to us and said, "Sorry, but we'll have to wrap this up early today. Mr. Pearson, you need to stick around."

Now, as I was sitting there and watching all of this take place, I didn't know what was on the fax sheet. It was only later that I found out what had happened. Someone had removed the Eastern Region chief as a witness. In his place they'd put Michael Bromwich, who was the Inspector General for the Department of Justice. The I.G. is one of the most powerful positions in the federal government. And the reason the I.G. had gotten involved was because, unbeknownst to the INS, investigators from the Inspector General's office had gone along the northern border and had done a secret report on staffing. That was why Michael Bromwich was coming in to back up my testimony and why Lamar Smith's office had told me not to worry because I'd be taken care of.

Of course, at the time, I didn't know what was going on behind the scenes. They'd just told me, "We'll see you in the morning."

Then the next morning, when I got to the hearing room, there were two guys from the Inspector General's office who'd been out to Blaine and whom I'd briefly talked to. The day they'd spoken to me in Blaine, I didn't know they were with the I.G.'s office. We'd talked about the Abu Mezer case, and I thought that they were simply two investigators from D.C.

Anyway, the Associate INS Commissioner, Michael Pearson, then gave his opening statement. To paraphrase his words, as best as I remember them: "It's a pleasure to be here, and I just want it on the record that we completely agree with Deputy Chief Davis that we need to put more Border Patrol agents on the northern border."

When I heard the Associate INS Commissioner say that, I could've fallen out of my chair. Then the Inspector General came in and testified. I remember it sort of felt like a heavy weight had been lifted off my shoulders. Both men had been respectful of my views.

Now, when I testified, Congresswoman Shelia Jackson Lee asked me my opinion as to how many additional patrol agents I thought we needed on the northern border. I said, "For our sector, I think we need another seventy-five agents."

And again, this was pre-9/11; and it was just a Congressional hearing. I knew that the opinions being presented probably wouldn't be quickly acted upon. Still, I was truly elated that Congress had finally been made aware of the needs of our northern border.

Also, as I had been promised, Lamar Smith's final question to me was about the Jordan Commission. He asked me if I thought there was any solution to illegal immigration.

I cleared my throat and said, "The only way to control illegal immigration in this country will not be done by just adding additional resources. We need E-Verify." I'm paraphrasing my words per my memory of what I said that day.

Then as I was walking out of the hearing room, a guy who was attached to the commissioner's office shuffled over to me. No one else was looking at us, and he said, "Out f***ing standing. Somebody finally got to say it. Congratulations. Thank you."

I honestly didn't know who he was. I think he might have either been an attorney or a senior staff officer.

So I came out of the hearing room feeling like I was ten feet tall. Yet sadly, as the months ticked by after my testimony, the members of Congress still didn't pass legislation to enforce E-Verify. But Congressman Lamar Smith at least tried to move his colleagues in that direction. He'd praised me for my testimony. He'd told me that he was aware of the benefits of E-Verify. But then later, as time had progressed, he'd gotten beaten back on it because the U.S. Chamber of Commerce and the low-wage business lobbyists had mounted such a strong campaign opposing the legislation.

It should also be pointed out that Lamar Smith and Barbara Jordan had represented separate congressional districts in Texas. He'd been a friend of hers, and he said that Barbara Jordan was one of the most highly respected people he'd ever had the pleasure of working with and that he'd read her report.

So I had testified at the hearing in April of 1999. Then what the Immigration Service did, during the last eight months that I worked for the Border Patrol before my retirement—was that the Commissioner of the Immigration Service, Doris Meissner, personally came to Blaine, WA, and held a community meeting. What the higher-ups had decided to do—instead of immediately giving us the new positions that we needed—was that they were going to give us 4.5 to 5 million dollars for a new pilot project. We were told that this money would be used to put cameras along the international border.

Consequently, Doris Meissner had a townhall meeting with most of the local Border Patrol agents and with the media. News reporters were brought in to generate press coverage in order to get the word out that Congress was increasing our country's surveillance along the northern border. And it wasn't just for show because the cameras actually did work.

At the meeting, Commissioner Meissner explained to those who had attended the townhall that this would be the first area on the northern border that would have a camera system. I had met Doris Meissner once before because she'd flown out to Scott's funeral. So, as one might imagine, it was an interesting townhall meeting because, not only were U.S. reporters there; but the Canadian media had also shown up, too. Needless to say, I knew most of the reporters.

I think 60% of the questions were probably fielded to me. The reporters would say things like, "Deputy Davis, do you really believe that the Border Patrol is sincere in doing this?"

I said, "Yes, I do."

And to Commissioner Meissner's credit, she was upfront and was willing to share a number of the details of the pilot program.

Yet since I was so close to retirement, the new cameras were put in after I had left the Border Patrol. I retired in January of 2000. I had a total of 30 years of government service, counting sick leave and military time. I had no desire to stay on any longer because of the sudden about-face in our enforcement duties. One of the issues which had really soured me was the fact that earlier that year, the higher-ups had decreed that the Border Patrol would strictly be "on the border." This meant that we would no longer do interior enforcement, such as reforestation, nor would we be working with the Forest Service.

So several of the important enforcement tools, which I had spent years focused on, were soon to be turned over to the district offices. In our sector's case, these duties would be transferred to the Immigration office down in Seattle and the other district office in Portland. Yet I knew those offices did not have the manpower or the staff to properly handle such investigations because I'd been an investigator in Seattle and the agents in that office didn't have the will to do what was required. They weren't going to go out and work 17 or 18 hours each day, 10 days straight like we did.

Of course, I had a fairly unique understanding of the overall picture when I advocated for additional resources on the northern border. Yet there was little I could do about the district personnel who weren't actually working at the border and who were simply attempting to manage the agency's manpower in order to increase our border coverage in other regions. It was a bitter pill to swallow because I'd spent so many years successfully improving our ability to apprehend illegal aliens in the interior—only to have those programs taken away from us. That about-face was too much for me to take. I had served my 30 years, and it was time for me to retire.

I had two weeks of sick leave that I hadn't used, and I was planning on just taking sick leave for the last two weeks of December. But then, on December 14th of 1999, we got the Millennium Bomber case in our sector at the Port Angeles ferry dock.

Ahmed Ressam was a person who'd entered Canada, years before, with a fraudulent passport. He was born in Algeria, and he spoke French. Ressam had moved to Montreal, where he was able to easily use his French language skills. It's also interesting to note that when Ahmed Ressam had first come into Canada, he'd immediately been intercepted by the Canadian authorities due to the fact that he had a passport with someone else's name on it. So the Mounties had actually known, early on, that his passport had been a forgery; but they had, for some reason, released him. Ressam then had proceeded to receive $550 a month as a refugee in Canada because he said he was afraid to go back to Algeria since he claimed his life would be in danger due to the war that was going on there. He also claimed that he didn't have any terrorist ties. His refugee status was almost a casebook example of how exceptionally liberal Canadian immigration actually was.

So once Ahmed Ressam was in Canada, he was allowed to remain. The Canadians didn't deport him. He eventually hooked up with a terrorist group that was based in Montreal. C.S.I.S.—the Canadian Security Intelligence Service, which is the Canadian equivalent of our CIA—had gotten suspicious of the group that Ahmed Ressam had joined; and C.S.I.S. began wiretapping their conversations.

A bit later, Ahmed Ressam met a recruiter who was working for al-Qaeda. And that was when he joined that much larger terrorist organization. He next stole a blank baptismal certificate and made up the name *Benni Noris* and used that official-looking document to get a legitimate Canadian passport with his photo in it. He then assumed the identity of *Benni Noris*, which was a person who didn't even exist. In other words, the Canadian authorities actually had Ahmed Ressam on their watchlist; but because they weren't aware of his new identity—*Benni Noris* wasn't a person of interest to them. So Ahmed Ressam had, more or less, completely disappeared.

With his new Canadian passport in hand, *Benni Noris* flew to Pakistan and went to Peshawar. He crossed the Khyber Pass and hooked up with an al-Qaeda operative, who took him to a terrorist training camp in Afghanistan. *Benni Noris* spent 11 months in two or three training camps. Al-Qaeda then recognized his ability to become a bombmaker, and he was introduced to Abu Zubaydah, who became his handler in Afghanistan.

Benni Noris's terroristic indoctrination continued as Zubaydah personally moved him from one training camp to another training camp. Then after *Noris* had been there for 11 months, he flew back to Canada via L.A.X. in Los Angeles. And since his passport appeared to be a valid document per his assumed identity—that was why the Canadian authorities weren't able to locate Ahmed Ressam because they didn't know about his fake persona as *Benni Noris.*

After he'd arrived back in Canada, *Noris* had about $12,000 in cash on him, along with a few bombmaking manuals and even some bombmaking materials. He'd also, by that point, already determined that he was going to bomb L.A.X., having seen how big that international airport was per his connecting flight. He had decided that it would be the perfect place to set off a bomb because of the huge number of people coming and going out of its terminals.

From L.A.X., *Benni Noris* flew to Vancouver, British Columbia. He spent a month or so looking around Vancouver, and then he flew back to Montreal. I'm not exactly sure how long he was in Montreal, but it was there that he hooked up with an associate who helped him sort through some of the details of his bomb plot. After a short while, the two of them then flew back to Vancouver, where they rented a hotel room.

In Vancouver they got the rest of the components that they needed to put a bomb together. *Noris* had four boxes he'd built with Casio watches as timing devices. His bombs were very sophisticated. He also knew exactly what chemicals he needed to build the bombs with. He had two big jars of nitroglycerin. His associate and him had cooked all of this stuff together in their hotel room in Vancouver, B.C.

Now, if a terrorist was going to bring a bomb into the United States from Vancouver, B.C.—the three logical places to transport such a device across the border would be through the truck crossing in Blaine, WA; or through Lynden, WA; or through Sumas, WA—which are the ports of entry in northwestern Washington State that are only a short distance south of Vancouver, British Columbia.

But that's not what *Benni Noris* did. He instead chose to come into the U.S. via a different route after his associate and him had built all of their bombmaking material. *Noris* drove a rental car onto the B.C. ferry from Vancouver to Victoria, British Columbia; and he then drove the rental car over to the Black Ball ferry terminal. The Black Ball—as it's called—is a car ferry that travels from Victoria, British Columbia, to Port Angeles, Washington. I suspect he chose Port Angeles because, at that disembarking point, they lacked outside computer terminals.

To conceal his bombmaking material, *Benni Noris*— a.k.a., Ahmed Ressam—had taken out the rental car's spare tire. He'd then hidden his boxes in the trunk's wheel well. To this day, we're still uncertain if his accomplice had ridden on the ferry with him or not. But if there was a second terrorist on the Black Ball that day, he wasn't in the car with Ressam.

Also, it should be noted that Victoria, B.C., was an interesting choice as an exit point from Canada. As I've explained in an earlier chapter, I had at one time worked in the Bahamas; and in Freeport they had pre-inspections for international travelers. So the U.S. immigration inspectors who were stationed in Victoria did the exact same thing. This meant that the Canadians weren't actually checking the cars that were leaving British Columbia, nor did we have U.S. Customs inspectors in Victoria. Our Customs officers did their inspections in Port Angeles, once the ferry had docked in Washington State.

So because *Benni Noris* had a valid Canadian passport, he didn't have any trouble clearing Immigration in Victoria in order to come to the U.S. He simply drove his rental car, a late-model Chrysler 300 sedan, onto the car ferry, which then cruised south across the Strait of Juan De Fuca and docked in Port Angeles. His rental car was the last car off the ferry, and there was a customs inspector who then walked up to the sedan's driver's side window and spoke to *Noris*. She was a really good inspector. Indeed, all of the inspectors at Port Angeles were very professional. That night I think there were only three inspectors working, and it would've been the last ferry to arrive on their p.m. shift. Also, there weren't a lot of cars which had driven off the Black Ball once it docked, as I understand it. So the traffic from Canada had been fairly light.

When the customs inspector first talked to *Noris*, he acted nervous. That's when she got suspicious and had him pull in for a secondary inspection—where she asked to see his identification and noticed that he spoke very little English. But instead of giving her his Canadian passport in the name of *Benni Noris*, he handed her his Costco card. Of course, such a card doesn't mean much, but he tried to use it as a means of identification.

The customs inspector then had him step out of his vehicle. As she began questioning him, another inspector—who she was working with—walked to the rear of the car and popped its trunk. When that inspector looked inside the trunk, all he saw was a suitcase and some travel items. But then as he opened up the wheel well, he noticed quite a few packages of white powder. Taking a closer look, he also found some timing devices, which were sitting beside two boxes of liquids. The chemicals didn't have any labels on their containers, and the inspector wasn't able to determine what type substances they were. He also found some white powder in two small bottles.

Becoming more and more concerned, the second customs inspector suspected that the unknown substances were drugs; and so that's when he alerted his fellow officers by hollering at them. "WE'VE GOT SOMETHING HERE!"

As this was happening, another customs inspector was patting *Benni Noris* down and going through the pockets of his jacket. Then all of a sudden, *Noris* slipped out of his jacket and took off running. He dashed out the door and left the customs inspector holding his jacket by the collar.

A couple of officers took off after him. But they momentarily lost him when he sprinted out into a line of traffic that was backed up on the other side of the ferry dock, which allowed him to quickly make his way into the city of Port Angeles.

After a few minutes, the officers finally caught up with him. They found him hiding underneath a vehicle. Then as they slowly approached him—he jumped up, dashed off again, and ran toward a stoplight.

Sitting in her car and waiting for the light to turn green, an older woman was startled when *Benni Noris* tried to get in her car. The lady got so frightened that she pressed down on the accelerator. As the car jerked forward, it prevented him from carjacking her vehicle. This slowed *Noris* down, and the two customs inspectors were able to tackle him to the ground.

When they brought him back to the customs station, that location didn't have a secure lock-up area to hold him in. So he was put in the back seat of a Port Angeles police car, which had a holding cage inside it.

While this was going on, another customs officer was doing a test on the chemicals that had been found in the rental car. The officer was convinced that the containers were filled with illegal drugs. As he was testing the liquids, *Noris* was still being held in the police car; and one of the officers noticed that he quickly ducked down in the back seat, looking as though he expected something was about to explode.

The officers later found out that a timing device had been hooked up but that it didn't have a detonator attached to it. Also, in addition to the nitroglycerin and the unknown powder, there was a chemical fertilizer inside one of the boxes, which was sometimes used to make an explosive. Plus, *Noris* had two little pill bottles with white powder inside each of them. One was a throat-lozenge bottle, and the other one was a headache-medicine bottle. If the investigative officer had stuck a spoon into one of those bottles, there was the possibility that it could've exploded. But at the time they didn't know that.

After a few more minutes had passed—the Border Patrol agent in charge of our Port Angeles office, Mike Baker, showed up. He was told by the customs inspectors that they thought they had it under control, and they thanked him for coming by. But then when they continued testing the chemicals which they'd found, they couldn't get the substances to test positive for drugs.

So that's when they contacted the U.S. Attorney's office. They explained the situation and proceeded to point out that they'd found what looked like timing devices, along with the unknown powder—which wouldn't test positive for drugs. Yet, as it turned out, they were talking on the phone to an inexperienced U.S. Attorney.

He asked them, "Have you identified a detonator?"

One of the customs inspectors replied, "No, we can't determine if there's a detonator, and we don't know what the other stuff is, either."

The U.S. Attorney said, "Well, I will not authorize you to lock the guy up. You're just going to have to seize all of those items and kick him loose."

Now, in the meantime, while all of this was taking place—the Coast Guard, Customs, and ATF had gotten involved. A Coast Guard helicopter had flown into Port Angeles from Bellingham, and several officers had begun going through all of the items that'd been found inside the rental car's trunk.

Then after the U.S. Attorney had decided not to have *Benni Noris* arrested, the ATF agent and the Customs agent that had arrived at the port of entry—who were both former Border Patrol agents—huddled together and discussed the situation. Coincidentally, the ATF agent had previously worked for me.

And so, from the legal knowledge they'd accrued per their years of Border Patrol experience, those two officers immediately knew that *Noris* could, in fact, be arrested on immigration charges. And that was when they talked to Mike Baker, and Mike immediately arrested *Benni Noris* on immigration charges.

I got two phone calls that night. One was from Mike Baker; and the other was from Keith Miller, who was the assistant chief under me. Keith was responsible for the Port Angeles station. Mike had called Keith and told him he'd arrested *Benni Noris*. Mike explained that *Noris* had been taken to the Border Patrol office—where he was processed and fingerprinted.

This was also when the I.B.E.T. team's interagency relationships, which we'd formed with our Canadian counterparts, had come into play because Mike Baker had a contact at the R.C.M.P. So Mike faxed *Benni Noris's* fingerprints to his Canadian contact, not knowing that the guy's real name was actually Ahmed Ressam.

Mike then proceeded to write *Noris* up, and we decided not to put any bond on him. We didn't want him to be released. We didn't want to take a chance on him bonding out.

Luckily for everyone involved, it didn't take long for the R.C.M.P. to run their fingerprint check.

BINGO!

The prints came back as belonging to Ahmed Ressam, not as those of *Benni Noris*. And because the C.S.I.S. had a file on him—that's when we knew, without any doubt whatsoever, he had terrorist ties. Plus, as Mike was processing him, Ressam claimed he was a French Canadian. But his English was so bad that Mike had to get a French-speaking interpreter on the phone as a third party. This was our regular procedure when we arrested someone since we were required to fill out a full report, which involved a good bit of detail.

Anyway, after about five minutes, the interpreter told Mike, "Get him off the phone a minute. I need to talk to you in private."

Mike then had Ressam hang up the phone that he was talking to the interpreter on.

The interpreter told Mike, "There's no way in the world this guy is a French Canadian. His accent is way off. I suspect he's an Algerian."

And, indeed, that was true. Ahmed Ressam was, in fact, an Algerian.

So we'd already arrested him, and he was now in our custody. It didn't take long for the FBI to send in their evidence team, which included a French-speaking agent from Seattle. The agent was able to talk to Ressam, without having to use a translator. The FBI then took over the case after we transported Ressam down to their Seattle office and officially turned him over to the Bureau.

In hindsight, I think there's an important lesson to be learned when we step back and look at how all of this had unfolded. Ahmed Ressam—a.k.a., *Benni Noris*—had crossed into the United States from Canada with bombmaking material. And, here again, this particular type of incident had been the kind of terrorist act which I'd been concerned about after I'd seen what had occurred with the Abu Mezer case a few years earlier. Back then, I'd said, "I don't think this will turn out to be a single event. I think we may have other terrorist activities which we should be worried about. I think we have every reason to suspect this isn't going to be an isolated incident."

So the Port Angeles bomb-smuggling attempt had happened on December 14th of 1999; and I'd been planning on taking two weeks of sick leave in order to end out my Border Patrol service and then retire. But as the public information officer for our sector, you can imagine how busy I suddenly got per having to deal with all of the inquiries as to what had happened—once the press had labeled Ahmed Ressam as the Millennium Bomber.

Also, we were very concerned that another similar event could surprise us since the terrorist bombing at L.A.X. was supposed to have taken place on January 1st, which would've been the first day of the new millennium, i.e., the first day of the year 2000.

So that was why I didn't take my sick leave. I instead hung on for two more weeks and continued working. It soon got pretty crazy because someone leaked a few of the particulars of the case to the media since we hadn't sent out a press release. Up until that point, we'd kept it hush-hush and hadn't told anyone about what had gone down for two days. I'm not sure, but I suspect someone at the FBI had leaked the info. Then all of a sudden, we were fielding call after call from reporters from across the country.

Now, let me just give you an example of how asinine things can get in this type of situation. People talk about the cooperation which exists amongst the federal agencies, such as tends to happen between the FBI and the Border Patrol. And per a general perspective—overall—the interface that's shared by such agencies is truly solid on many levels.

Yet what I didn't explain in regards to when Ahmed Ressam had been apprehended after he'd driven off the ferry from Victoria, B.C.—was that C.S.I.S. had flown two officers in on a helicopter from Canada to Port Angeles while we were still processing Ressam. I was only later told this nugget of information by one of the agents who was there that day and who had previously worked for me.

The agent had also gone on to explain that the customs inspectors in Port Angeles had been trying to determine what the chemical powders were in Ressam's rental car and that the ATF agent who'd arrived on the scene had decided to fly the chemicals down by plane to Walnut Creek, California—where the ATF's forensic lab was located.

But because the visibility was so bad that day, their agency's plane couldn't fly in to pick up the chemicals. So that's when two ATF agents drove nonstop with the two pill containers down to the Walnut Creek lab in order for their technicians to be able to extract the needed samples and thus perform a forensic test. Then after the ATF agents had allowed the lab workers at Walnut Creek to extract the samples, the two of them had immediately turned around and had headed back up to their office, taking the rest of the chemicals in the pill containers with them. But just as they crossed the Oregon/Washington border, their pagers and phones went off.

They were told, "Be very careful. Take the pill containers to a bunker. Those are chemical explosives, which are a powderized rocket propellent that can be used as a detonator."

And so that was what had happened with the two ATF agents when they had unknowingly put their lives at risk.

Also, when the FBI rolled into town, the Bureau's agents did the typically thing that the FBI does. They brought the guy from the ATF in; they brought the guy from Customs in—and, like I've already mentioned, the two guys from C.S.I.S. were also there.

One of the FBI agents said to the ATF agent, "What have you got?"

The ATF agent then explained everything he had. But he was also pissed off since he'd stored all of the evidence he'd gathered up in the Customs office safe, and it'd been taken out by the FBI.

The FBI agent then turned to the Customs officer and asked him what he had.

The Customs officer explained what he'd found out about *Benni Noris*. And based upon this feedback and what had happened, the FBI claimed that Ahmed Ressam was going to drive the explosives all the way down to Los Angeles. But then when the Customs agent had checked with the airlines, he'd found out that Ressam—under the name of *Benni Noris*—had booked a confirmed reservation the following night to fly from Seattle to New York and then from New York to London. And, of course, there's more collateral information such as this, which can't be discussed due to its sensitive nature.

Also, after the FBI agent had spoken to the ATF and Customs officers, he then asked the two C.S.I.S. agents, "What have you got?"

Up until that point, the C.S.I.S. guys hadn't actually identified Ahmed Ressam to their U.S. counterparts. So that was when one of the C.S.I.S. officers said to the FBI, "No, you go first. What have you got?"

Tensing up, the FBI agent shook his head and said, "Look, I'm sorry; but we can't tell you that. It's classified information."

Then one of the C.S.I.S. guys replied, "You don't tell us; we don't tell you. We can play that same game."

And so, like I stated, there was an asinine element as to how these two law enforcement officers—who were basically on the same side—interacted with each other. Then when the two guys from C.S.I.S. were about to walk out the door, one of them pulled the ATF agent and the Customs agent over and said, "Listen, boys, let me tell you something. This thing is f**king big. The bomber's real name is Ahmed Ressam. He came directly out of the terrorist training camps in Afghanistan. This thing is big."

And the Canadian Security Intelligence Service agent was absolutely right. The Millennium Bomber plot was, indeed, a huge *red flag*.

So later, when the French-speaking FBI agent had established a rapport with Ressam and Ressam had finally come clean, he'd told the FBI agent where he'd been living while he was overseas. But at that time, no one had ever heard of Abu Zubaydah; and that was how Zubaydah had first been identified by law enforcement. Ressam had coughed up Abu Zubaydah's identity.

Then after the tragic events of 9/11, which had occurred 21 months subsequent to Ressam's appre- hension, Zubaydah had left Afghanistan and had traveled to Rawalpindi in Pakistan. He was eventually shot and wounded in Faisalabad. And, to the best of my knowledge, I think the overt operation to track him down had been initiated by a combined effort of the CIA and the Pakistani Intelligence. Zubaydah had almost been killed. But luckily, they were able to capture him.

When he was later interrogated, he identified Khalid Sheikh Mohammed as the 9/11 mastermind.

So the C.S.I.S. agent had been absolutely right when he'd said that Ahmed Ressam's capture had been a really big deal. The future implications were, in fact, extremely important to our national security.

Consequently, the Border Patrol had done its part. We had arrested *Benni Noris*, and he was held in custody until we could turn him over to the FBI.

Now, as one would imagine, after a few details of Ressam's arrest were leaked—the media was everywhere. Dozens of reporters were asking all sorts of questions. So my boss, Carey James, did not want me to retire because I was the station's P.I.O. guy.

Then while this press feeding frenzy was going on, an Iranian—who'd been living illegally in the United States—had paid money to have his wife, legitimately, flown into Vancouver, B.C. Someone had agreed to illegally walk her across the border, and she was arrested by the Border Patrol. A few of the reporters got wind of the story because she was from Iran, and they erroneously tied it to terrorism.

So one morning, when I called the office to see if I had any messages, it turned out that I had 35 messages on my answering machine. Then when I drove to Blaine, I had a bunch of media people waiting for me. They wanted to know about the Iranian whom we'd brought in during the previous night because they had presumed he was part of the Millennium Bomber plot. A few of the reporters had even gone over to the Customs office to check on the status of the Iranian, and they'd been kicked out of the Customs office because they were being so pushy. Plus, no one could answer any of their questions.

I told the reporters, "Look, you guys go get a cup of coffee. I'll go find out what we've got. Come back in an hour, and I'll have a briefing."

And that's what the reporters did. They came back in an hour; and I told them, "This is not a terrorism case. This is just a case which we typically get every now and then."

In other words, the Iranian husband-and-wife situation was of little consequence to the press. They were wasting their time trying to cover it.

Then once that tempest in a teapot had blown over, I ended up retiring on December 31st, 1999. I worked the 4 p.m.-to-midnight shift. I'd decided to stay onboard until the new millennium had arrived in order to see if something else unexpected would happen. Also, Patrick McMahon—a reporter from *USA Today* who'd written a number of stories about terrorist attacks—was up on the border that night. He came in my office, and we shot the bull until midnight.

When New Year's Day was ushered in on that Friday morning, nothing happened. Then the following Monday, I turned in my badge. So I guess, in one respect, I went out on a high note since the Millennium Bomber had been stopped and no one had been blown up. I certainly felt vindicated as to the suspicions I'd had in regards to maintaining the security of our northern border.

A few months after I had retired, one of the intelligence guys called me and told me that they'd stopped getting directives from the regional office which forbid them from submitting the so-called *T-reports*. It was nice to learn that my efforts to improve our national security had not been in vain.

# # #

EUGENE DAVIS

With over 30 years of government service, Eugene Davis retired from the U.S. Border Patrol as the Deputy Chief of the Blaine sector in NW Washington State. In 1971 he began his career as a journeyman agent on the U.S.-Mexico border and later transferred up to the Canadian border, where he subsequently helped manage the successful response to the Millennium Bomber terrorist case and the initial apprehension of the Brooklyn Bomber—who'd been intent on blowing up a NYC subway. Over the many years of Deputy Chief Davis's exemplary career, he received numerous outstanding-service commendations from his INS superiors, along with several letters of appreciation from the FBI for his exceptional number of apprehensions per a series of coordinated law enforcement efforts with the Justice Department. Deputy Chief Davis was also instrumental in the formulation of the very first Integrated Border Enforcement Team with Canada; and he testified before several Congressional committees in regards to illegal immigration and the need for enhanced border security, earning him thank you letters from Congressman Lamar Smith and Senator Carl Levin.